Patriarch of
the American Frontier

Patriarch of the American Frontier

The Life of Reverend Father Elisha John Durbin

Donald R. Durbin, Jr.

iUniverse, Inc.
New York Lincoln Shanghai

Patriarch of the American Frontier
The Life of Reverend Father Elisha John Durbin

Copyright © 2004, 2007 by Donald R. Durbin, Jr.

All rights reserved. No part of this book may be used or reproduced by any means, graphic, electronic, or mechanical, including photocopying, recording, taping or by any information storage retrieval system without the written permission of the publisher except in the case of brief quotations embodied in critical articles and reviews.

iUniverse books may be ordered through booksellers or by contacting:

iUniverse
2021 Pine Lake Road, Suite 100
Lincoln, NE 68512
www.iuniverse.com
1-800-Authors (1-800-288-4677)

The views expressed in this work are solely those of the author and do not necessarily reflect the views of the publisher, and the publisher hereby disclaims any responsibility for them.

ISBN: 978-0-595-30294-9 (pbk)
ISBN: 978-0-595-66149-7 (cloth)

Printed in the United States of America

Contents

Preface	Patriarch of the American Frontier	vii
Chapter 1	Blind Johnny	1
Chapter 2	Big Joe	32
Chapter 3	A Boone to Society	41
Chapter 4	The Primordial	52
Chapter 5	Methodist in the Midst	63
Chapter 6	The Ministry	71
Chapter 7	The Tangled Webb	102
Chapter 8	The Letter "K"	130
Chapter 9	Pierre-Jean De Smet	138
Chapter 10	The Sunset	143
	Sources	171

Preface

My mother, Dorothy May (Schmitzer) Durbin Breitenbach (1914-1990) often expressed her desire to write a book about *The Patriarch Priest of Kentucky*, Father Elisha John Durbin, the Roman Catholic priest who was also known as *The Apostle of Western Kentucky*.

(From here on I will refer to my mother as *Dorothy*.) Dorothy was an author in her own rite, having published numerous stories in Catholic and other publications, notably the *Catholic Weekly, Immaculata, Our Sunday Visitor, the Catholic Digest, Scope, The Christian, Grits, Guideposts, The Detroit News,* and *Good Old Days*. Besides devoting extensive time and effort to writing, she spent roughly thirty years of her life researching Durbin families. She developed a fascination with the historical significance of the Durbin name and had a burning desire to learn what made her husband, Donald Ross Durbin, "tick." In researching the Durbins, taking great pains to document and authenticate everything, she traveled to all the places where she knew there was some Durbin ancestry. Her research took her to such places as Kentucky, Ohio, Maryland, and even England.

A devout Catholic herself, Dorothy's research of Durbin and related families made her ideally suited to write a book about Father Durbin. I can only wish that she would have had done just that. (I studied for the priesthood for a short while, but that does not make me any more qualified to write this story.) The following pages constitute a book, a story about Father Durbin that must be told. This saintly frontier priest outranked most of the clerics of his day, not only in the high esteem in which his parishioners and others held him, but also in the extent and endurance of his frontier journeyings.

In the work that follows, unless otherwise noted, the information is the result of Dorothy's research, augmented by some of my own.

Being a Durbin myself, I am most prejudiced and proud to have ancestors who produced such an impact on the lives of Americans as did Father Durbin.

Some of this pride is exemplified in my recent book about my mother's grandfather, William Peter Burfening. The book, entitled *The Bigger They Are...*, chronicles Mr. Burfening's lifelong fight with a railroad company in Minnesota. He, like Father Durbin, was a man of courage and perseverance.

Father Durbin is my second cousin, four generations removed, and our common ancestor is Samuel S. Durbin (1704-1752). Father Durbin's grandfather, Christopher Durbin (1741-1825), son of Samuel Durbin, was an early pioneer in Kentucky. Samuel Durbin and his wife, Ann Logsdon (1723 to about 1777) are the common ancestors of most, if not *all* of the Durbins in the United States. Samuel Durbin descended from Thomas Durbin, the first documented Durbin in America, who sailed from Bristol, England in 1663.

Europeans were especially fascinated by the New World in the late eighteenth and early nineteenth centuries. No one seemed to be more curious, however, than Vatican authorities. They knew very little about the United States, and bishops and priests often wrote to Rome describing the American nation and, particularly, the state of Catholicism in this country. These documents constitute a very important source for understanding the early history of American Catholicism when it was still basically a mission Church surpassed in numbers and even importance by many European dioceses.

Even though there was an acute shortage of clergy in the early days of the United States, adventursome Americans of English and Irish descent began pushing the frontier westward. The majority of these pioneers clung to their Catholic heritage, attending Mass and the sacraments whenever they could, sometimes travelling many, many miles on horseback to attend Mass. Fasting preparatory to receiving Holy Communion began at midnight the day before the Mass, and many of these pioneers and their family members sometimes had eaten no food for almost a whole day. Father Durbin eventually helped to ease the burden on the early Kentucky Catholics.

For many centuries before the arrival of the white man, the Kentucky region was a hunting ground and battlefield for such Indian tribes as the Shawnee from the north and the Cherokee from the south. Even earlier agricultural and hunting peoples left burial mounds and other traces. French and Spanish explorers must have seen Kentucky from the rivers of the Mississippi basin, and traders entered the region from the eastern colonies during the early 18th century. In the 1750s and 1760s, the impediments offered by both the Indians and the complex physical geography of the region made serious attempts at exploration relatively unsuccessful. In 1769 Daniel Boone penetrated to the central plateau region, the present-day Bluegrass country.

Settlement was rapid in the 1770s, though the prophecies of an angry Cherokee chieftain named Dragging-Canoe—that Boone and other whites would find Kentucky "a dark and bloody land"—were in large part fulfilled. British officers spurred the Indians during the Revolution, notably in raids on Boonesboro in 1777 and 1778 and at a bloody ambush at Blue Licks in 1782, and settlers encountered numerous other sieges, scalpings, and skirmishes. Following the war, immigrants poured down the rivers and traveled the Wilderness Road from Cumberland Gap. The settlers founded towns, and before long began to call for separation of the judicial district of Kentucky from Virginia. Statehood conventions at Danville in the 1780s were somewhat ruffled by the *Spanish Conspiracy* of James Wilkinson and others to ally the region with Spain, but they led ultimately to admission into the Union on June 1, 1792, and to the organization of state government, which took place in a Lexington tavern.

Events leading to a second state constitution in 1800 revealed an internal division that continued to characterize Kentucky and create an unusual interest throughout the state in national politics. Farmers, who floated their grain, hides, and other products on flatboats down the Mississippi to Spanish-held New Orleans, allied themselves with other antislavery forces to oppose slaveholders and businessmen. The U.S. Alien and Sedition Acts of 1798, passed in an attempt to control criticism of the federal government, were vigorously opposed. One of the leading spokesmen for the opposition was the young politician Henry Clay, who was to stamp his personality on the state and national scenes as the "great compromiser" until his death in 1852.

Kentucky took a lead in the War of 1812, much of which was fought in the adjacent Northwest Territory against combined British and Indian forces. Following the war, a land boom, with attendant speculation and inflation, and the chartering of 40 independent banks that flooded the state with paper money led to financial disaster during the national economic panic of 1819. Fierce controversy over relief to debtors split Clay's Whigs and Andrew Jackson's Democrats. Signs of progress from 1820 to 1850, however, included the building of a canal at Louisville, the chartering of railroads, and increased manufacturing. The slavery question was uppermost, however, until the Civil War. The few large slaveholders were located mainly in the plantation agriculture of the Bluegrass and Pennyrile sections in western Kentucky, but by 1833, when the legislature forbade importation of slaves for resale, the state was already one-quarter black. Until the Civil War, pro-slavery forces maintained an iron control on government and prevented any constitutional change that might endanger their property. Much of the foregoing historical sketch was found in *The New Encyclopaedia Britannica Micropaedia.*

As a boy, Elisha John Durbin's desire to enter the priesthood was inspired by his local parish priest, Father Angier of St. Francis church in Scott County,

Kentucky. Father Angier spoke highly of young Elisha. As soon as he was old enough, Elisha entered the preparatory seminary of St. Thomas over in Nelson County. Seminary life in early Kentucky was extremely difficult, especially for Elisha John Durbin, for he was of small stature for a young man of high school age. About half of the seminary's curriculum consisted of manual labor, performing such tasks as gardening, groundskeeping and building maintenance. Although it must not have seemed so at the time, there was good reason for making such labor a part of a seminarian's school life. The outlying parts of Kentucky were wooded and wild. A priest had to be able to take care of himself in this wilderness.

Primarily due to the shortage of clergy, seminarians were ordained as priests as quickly as possible. In the rush to place priests in the leading edges of America's western frontiers, there were many compromises. Theological instruction was emphasized; however, school terms were shortened and this fact did leave some of the graduates a little less scholastically skilled than their fellow priests. The seminary acquired a dispensation to allow Father Durbin to be ordained at a younger age than was required by the Church. He became a priest at the age of twenty-two and went on to serve the people of Kentucky and parts of Tennessee, Illinois and Indiana for the next 65 years.

Father Elisha John Durbin, sometimes affectionately called *Daddy*, was a man of tremendous personal physical and spiritual strength and stamina. By the end of his nearly lifelong ministry he estimated that he had traveled more than half a million miles on horseback. His horses were always white, not unlike the Lone Ranger's horse. Over time, Father Durbin developed a craggy appearance because of the outdoor exposure to rain and sunlight, and hot and cold weather. In spite of this exposure, he was rarely sick. On his journeys he would stay overnight at the homes of his parishioners, sometimes saying Mass outdoors or inside a parishoner's home. (An outdoor Mass would be considered somewhat of a novelty today, but in Father Durbin's time it was often a necessity.) Through the course of his ministry, but mostly in its earlier days, he either personally built, or caused to be built, at least fifteen churches. During the Civil War his priority was attending to the souls of both the Union and Confederate soldiers. He was a saintly man by most definitions. As far as is known, no miracles are directly attributed to him, but the hard work he performed in very hard conditions is miraculous in itself.

Following her untimely death on Easter Sunday in 1990, I continued my mother's genealogy work, attempting to complete and publish it. As I accumulated family information over the years, the data grew to contain information on nearly 27,000 people; so publishing the genealogy would be almost impossible. However, this wealth of information does lend itself to creating individual stories. *Patriarch Of The American Frontier* represents a brief hiatus from the tiring and time-consuming work of organizing Dorothy's research notes. I have to appreciate the patience of my wife, Lynn, my brothers Bill and Jim, and that of all the hundreds of family members awaiting the result. I dedicate the meager effort contained herein to the memory of my mother.

Chapter 1

Blind Johnny

A considerable period prior to the admission of Kentucky into the Union, one reads among the names of the early Catholic settlers in Madison County, those of Durbin and Logsdon.

For two generations these families had been blessed with the light of the holy religion. The providential intermarriage of a member of one of them with a pious Catholic Irish girl, named Honor O'Flynn, had illumined the faith in the parents and children of both, previous to their migration to Kentucky. They were of a hardy, determined race, high in spirit, and strong in thew and sinew, fit pioneers to the land whither they went to abide, with the conditions which then encircled it. In the closing years of the eighteenth century we find living in Madison county John D. Durbin and Patience Logsdon, his wife, and on the first day of February 1800 was born their son, Elisha J. Durbin, called Elisha after a maternal ancestor.

The Reverend Father Elisha John Durbin, the *Patriarch priest of Kentucky*, was born at St. Christopher Mission February 1, 1800, in the Covington, Kentucky diocese in Richmond, Madison County, about sixteen miles above Boonesboro, and he had three brothers and four sisters. He was the son of John J. "Blind Johnny" Durbin (Mr. Steve Barr's notes indicate he was blind, and W. Jesse Durbin said his nickname was "Blind Johnny" or sometimes "Blind Uncle Johnny." How he lost his eyesight is not known.). One of Dorothy's correspondents said that this John Durbin was killed in the Civil War, but that would have been unlikely if he was blind, unless he was somehow accidentally killed as a civilian. His date of death is unknown. Father

Durbin's mother was Patience Logsdon, who was referred to in the Catholic Encyclopedia, Volume 5 (Kalamazoo, Michigan Library), as the mother of Father Elisha John Durbin. Father Durbin died in 1887 at Shelbyville, Kentucky.

Although it is a digression, we cannot refrain (in noticing how much the life of him who is now gone linked us with the past) to note that at the time of his nativity the population of the then fast developing city reached but three hundred and fifty nine souls.

Parents whose Catholicity was of a practical character, and whose lives were exemplary brought up the young Elisha. His boyhood's earliest aim was towards the hopes of better, and less material advantages, still he cheerfully wrought in the daily toil associated with the pioneer life of the family.

Born on the eve of the Purification, his faith in the intercession of the Virgin was boundless, and his prayer to her unstaying, and he had also throughout his life a fervent devotion to her chaste spouse, in the church dedicated to whose honor he was in later years, ordained.

When a boy he attended church with his parents at St. Francis' Church in Scott County. The pastor then was Reverend Robert Angier, O.S.D. who spoke in terms of endearment of him. (Reverend Angier took charge of St. Francis Church in 1808 according to Webb's history.)

According to some accounts, young Elisha began his studies for the priesthood at the age of sixteen at the Dominican College of St. Thomas at St. Rose in Washington County in pursuit of the studies preparatory for the priesthood. He passed six years in the seminary, half of the time in study and half the time labor. That was the rule of the seminary. However, he discovered that his vocation was not with the Order of Preachers, so in 1816 he was sent to the preparatory seminary of St. Thomas, in Nelson County, where he spent about four years of manual labor and study under such distinguished missionaries as David Flaget, Felix de Andreis, and Joseph Rosati. All seminarians performed manual labor in an effort to prepare them for the rigors of life they would experience after ordination. This labor included grounds maintenance, cooking, cleaning and the like. From there he went to the nearby Seminary of St. Joseph, at Bardstown, where, in 1821-1822, he had as an instructor Francis Patrick Kenrick, later Bishop of Philadelphia and Archbishop of Baltimore.

He was impelled to the Seminary of Saint Thomas by a vocation from above. In the Catholic Advocate, October 9, 1875, E. Blanca writes:

> His vocation was remarkable and truly apostolic. In his own simple fashion he relates how Father Fenwick, afterwards the first Bishop of Cincinnati, paid a pastoral visit to his father's place, and asked the old man if any of his sons showed an

inclination to study for the Church; and how, on the same occasion, while they were cutting and binding their oats in the field, his father mentioned the matter to him, remarking that he would like to get his answer before Father Fenwick left. Not wishing to be hurried in such a momentous affair, young Elisha Durbin asked to be allowed time to consider; and this delay materially influenced his destination, and perhaps changed his sphere of ministerial usefulness; for not having gone to the Dominican convent of Saint Rose, of which Father Fenwick was a member, he was sent soon after to the old diocesan seminary of Saint Thomas, Bardstown, and thus his lot was cast with the secular clergy of his native state.

At the seminary, as Father Durbin himself tells us, it was an uphill struggle in those primitive times, the students' daily occupation being an intermixture of snatches of study and necessary commonplace work. And cheerfully and perseveringly did he and his comrades—such as the energetic Father Abell and Father Reynolds, afterwards Bishop of Charleston, co-laborers in the Lord's vineyard, Father Hutchins, Commes, and Aud, show themselves willing and earnest In the various tasks allotted. It fell to Father Durbin's share to drive a weighty wagon filled with building materials to and fro over a creek, for the erection of the college, house, and church; and on one occasion, by some mishap, he allowed the whole load to topple over into the water. The foreman looked on with amazement at the coolness and unconcern with which he regarded the accident, expecting, probably to hear the boy break off with some strong expletives expressive of his anger, as is common in such cases.

He relates how he dug with his own hands the two first graves at Nazareth and Bardstown, religious institutions, and when he was first ordained, he walked three miles to the convent of morning to relieve his ecclesiastical superior, Bishop David, who was then busily engaged in perfecting the foundations and organization of the now well-known and most excellent religious community of the Sisters of Charity of Nazareth. For some months he remained at the Cathedral and taught at Saint Joseph's College. Having been sent afterwards on the Kentucky mission, he made his headquarters at the Church of the Sacred Heart, Union County, to which he was attached for forty-eight years without intermission of any sort. During this long interval his range of apostolic employment and pastoral attendance extended through that vast region—then unexplored and uncivilized—which lies between the Green and Tennessee Rivers; his ministrations were given, not unfrequently in Indiana and Illinois and portions of Tennessee. His parish comprised twenty-six distant and widely scattered stations.

Bishop David, who emigrated from France to become one of America's first priests, ordained Elisha in Bardstown on September 21, 1822. For over a year his duties held him to St. Joseph College and the cathedral church of the same name in Bardstown, Nelson County. The newly ordained priest served as a teacher at St. Joseph College, and then was assigned as an assistant at St. Joseph Cathedral until 1824. Early in 1824 Bishop Flaget entrusted him to the pastoral care of western and southwestern Kentucky, about thirty counties, with an area of over 11,000 square miles, nearly one-third of the State. Then began a missionary career of over sixty years hardly paralleled in the United States, and that subsequently won for him the names of *Apostle of Western Kentucky* and *Patriarch Priest of Kentucky*.

When Father Durbin reached the seat of his mission he found there a chapel of logs built upon the grounds of the Sisters of Charity of Nazareth at their establishment known then and still as the Academy of St. Vincent. The center of his mission was Union County. From it he journeyed on horseback over his vast territory, erected churches, established stations, formed congregations, and visited isolated families. In the beginning duty called him beyond his mission proper into Indiana, and once a year to Nashville, Tennessee. Always riding a white horse, he traversed his extensive and sparsely settled mission incessantly for over sixty years, his churches, stations, and the rude homes of his poor flock his only abiding places. Occasionally a communication from him would appear in the press, and then only in defence of truth or outraged justice. When he did write, he wrote cogently and elegantly.

On Father Durbin's arrival in the county, there was but one lonely hut that had the name of the "House of God," and one single school conducted by religious. These were the Sacred Heart Church and Saint Vincent Academy.

At once the zealous missionary girded himself to the holy work of erecting a fitting house of worship but relaxed a moment from his other labors. The new building stood close by the site of the old log chapel on the grounds of the Sisters of Charity. (Father Nerinckx had called this the "Oratory of the Sacred Hearts.")

The Catholic Miscellany tells us that Right Reverend Joseph Flaget, on his episcopal visitation, September 14, 1828, the anniversary of the Exaltation of the Holy Cross, blessed it. The same article also says:

> After the consecration of the Sacred Heart, the Bishop continued his episcopal visitation to the few congregations who could not partake of the Jubilee. He proceeded from Sacred Heart to Mount Carmel, a distance of ninety miles. The next stops were Saint James, Clifty Creek, Sandy Creek, Sunfish Creek, Leitchfield, Nolan Creek and Bear Creek. In these small congregations there were 310 communions.
>
> Saint James is the main church. They are erecting one at Clifty. At Saint Ignatius and Saint Clare the number of people was so great, the audience was addressed from a stand erected in the woods near the churches. Thus was concluded the visitation of the State of Kentucky. The Jubilee communicants numbered 5000.

These were golden days for the church In Kentucky. What had been but a few short years before, a vast and unreclaimed wilderness, inhabited only by the wild beast and the yet fiercer savage, had now become a blooming garden of Christianity in which flowers of piety sent forth their sweet fragrance, and in which the fruits of virtue were gathered in abundance. The hand of God rules over all.

What greater blessing could come to a congregation or to a home than to have a member become "a priest of God." Needless to say, therefore, there was general rejoicing when in the early days of 1828, young Charles Cissell became Union County's first priest. His mission was Saint Anthony. He acted as chaplain to the Loretta Sisters, then residing at the monastery *Mount Carmel*, where the Sisters of Charity had made a beginning in 1820, but had to leave before the year was up because the illness of Father Abell had left them without a pastor.

The points in the Owensboro diocese and elsewhere where Catholics were more numerous were Caseyville, Fancy Farm, Marquette, Dycusbury, Eddyville and Flint Island; in Illinois, Shawneetown and Carmi; in Indiana, Mount Vernon and Evansville.

Ben Webb gives Reverend R. E. Clark as Father Durbin's first assistant in 1829. Still Father Durbin's round of duties was the same. The population of his immediate district increased and required more visits; and spiritual aid was needed in places where Catholics had not lived before. It was about this time he established the congregation of Saint Ambrose. A few years later the Church of Saint Ambrose was built, known as "The Lower Chapel."

After 1824 and up to 1833, Ben Webb states, Reverend E. J. Durbin visited the Catholic people of Daviess County at long intervals from Union or by one of his assistants. Saint Lawrence was put up in 1831. Reverend J. C. Wathen became pastor in 1833, relieving Father Durbin of many missions in Daviess, Hardinsburgh and Meade Counties.

As the church grew, Father Durbin was relieved of the care of one and another of his farther removed outlying missions. His rides were not so long but his lank figure and bronzed face were as frequently seen on the road. He followed the straying sheep and brought them back to the fold.

Afterwards Father Durbin had his heart set on building a church at Fancy Farm In Graves County. He strove with hope to build it, and his energy was crowned with success; he saw it blessed under the invocation of Saint Jerome in the year 1836. Its first resident pastor was Father Hogan in 1843.

Saint Jerome had been previously attended from the Sacred Heart, and after the death of the resident pastor in 1848 it was again served by either Father Durbin or his second assistant in the mission, Reverend Stephen Ward.

Father Durbin or his assistant also attended the German families near Saint John.

One who lived until recently tells of Father Durbin's first visit. A band of men were cutting timber nearby when Father came riding along and asked if there were any Catholics in that neighborhood. Four of the timbermen came forward. One, a Mr. William Greif, invited Father Durbin to his home. Here the first Mass was said.

Before his departure from Saint John's, the congregation made up $5.00 to buy Father a new hat. On leaving, one remarked,

> I'll bet he doesn't get a hat, but gives the $5.00 to the first poor person he meets on the road.

Enfeebled by age, his sturdy constitution gave way in 1884, when his bishop, yielding to his entreaties, assigned him the small mission at Princeton, Kentucky. After a stroke of paralysis in 1885, he was given the chaplaincy of an academy at Shelbyville, Kentucky, where he later died.

Much of the preceding information was compiled by Louis G. Deppen and transcribed by Christine J. Murray. It was obtained from the Catholic Encyclopedia (copyright © 1913 by the Encyclopedia Press, Inc. Electronic version copyright © 1996 by New Advent, Inc.).

As noted in the following narrative, Father Durbin was truly of pioneer stock. His grandfather, Christopher Durbin, was one of the first settlers in Kentucky, having moved there from Maryland around 1785 after patriotic service in the Revolutionary War in Maryland according to researcher Mrs. Evalou Gillock. In the *History of the Covington Diocese* (page 62) it states that Durbins, of Irish descent, were the oldest family in the Covington Diocese, having come to Kentucky from Maryland by way of North Carolina. In reality, though, the Durbins were English and evidently came directly to Kentucky from Maryland, possibly with short stays in the neighboring territories. Kentucky became our 15th state in 1792.

Reverend Theodore Badin was the co-founder, with Father Nerinckx, of Catholicism in Kentucky. Before a church was built in Madison County, Father Badin said Mass at the home of Christopher Durbin. When the first church was built there in 1805, it became known as St. Christopher, the patron saint of Elisha Logsdon who is mentioned below. At that time there were only 23 Catholic families there. The following historical sketch was found in the Archives of the University of Notre Dame.

The first Catholics who traveled to Kentucky settled at Harrodsburg in 1775, and it was not until ten years later, in 1785, that Basil Hayden led the first colony of Catholics into Kentucky and established the Pottinger Creek settlement. (Basil Hayden eventually built a distillery in 1796 to manufacture bourbon whiskey. It was said that his bourbon was of very superior quality. There is a Kentucky bourbon sold yet today that bears his name, and it is very expensive, perhaps attesting to its fine quality. Basil Hayden died in 1804.) In 1791, under the leadership of Reverend William DeRohan, who had come with a group from North Carolina, the Pottinger Creek Catholics built a chapel, which was the first Catholic place of worship in Kentucky.

Joseph Clark is a leading authority on this period of time. According to Mr. Clark, "**All of the original priests assigned to the Mission of Chicago also attended to the needy along the Illinois and Michigan Canal, particularly the Haytown Mission, the original Illinois Canal Mission. This mission was later relocated to Lockport, Illinois, and dedicated as Saint Dennis Church. Joseph J. Thompson, editor of the Illinois Catholic Historical Review during the 1920's, referred to the original priests as 'Holy Tramps'. The 'Holy Tramps' labored spiritually and physically side by side with the pioneer builders of Mid-America, fulfilling the vision of Marquette and Jolliet. The toils of the pioneer builders, predominantly Irish immigrant laborers, built the canal that would give birth to the mighty megalopolis of Chicago. To better understand the constitution of the missionaries who ventured to the canal chapel at Haytown, a sketch of the American proto-priest, the good Sulpician Father Stephen Theodore Badin, must be drawn, especially since he was a mentor to Father Elisha Durbin.**"

Mr. Clark also notes, "Father Badin was the first priest ordained in the United States by Bishop John Carroll at Baltimore. He was happy to announce that he was the "proto sacerdos" (first priest). On May 25, 1793, a career of exalted devotion commenced which would move and inspire generations of priests and laity alike. Until late in his life Father Badin roved continuously across Kentucky, Indiana, Ohio, Michigan and Illinois. His first mission of thirty-seven years was to the state of Kentucky." Along with being in the Chicago area, in 1830 Father Badin went to Niles, Michigan, to assume control of Saint Joseph's Indian School. His calling would involve extensive work with indigenous tribes, particularly the Potawatomi tribe. It was through his interactions with the natives that Father Badin arranged a land grant near Chicago in 1831 for a Catholic college. Although all parties connected signed the pact, the tract of land near Irving Park Road and the Des Plaines River was never developed."

Finally, Mr. Clark goes on to state, "More important, Father Badin did negotiate the land grant in 1837, which was a success. This land was transferred to the Bishop of Vincennes for the purpose of breaking ground for a college. As a result Bishop Hailandiére donated the site to Father Edward Sorin for the establishment of Notre Dame Du Lac at South Bend, Indiana. Father Badin is considered the founding benefactor of that institution."

Notre Dame University was founded in 1842. It is located just north of South Bend, Indiana and is probably best known today for its football history. By some reports, the Notre Dame football team invented the forward pass and they put on a sensational exhibition in defeating Army in the inaugural game of their rivalry in 1913 at West Point. Army chose to play Notre Dame to fill a vacant spot in their football schedule. The game was expected to be an easy pleasant afternoon sport for the home team. Notre Dame's frolics and football meant nothing to the East Coast teams at that time. Quarterback Gus Dorais threw to Knute Rockne, later the most famous coach in football history, and to back Joe Pliska. Notre Dame completely surprised the Army team by scoring an astonishing 35-13 victory over the cadets and their old-style battering ram running game. Later that same season Army used the forward pass against Navy and won 22-9. It turns out that Notre Dame was not the trailblazer its performance made it appear to be. Several teams used the forward pass since it was adopted in 1906.

Today, Notre Dame University is widely regarded as the leading Roman Catholic University in the United States. Many of its faculty members have been recognized at the national level, and this helped to overcome Notre Dame's image as an institution solely devoted to athletics. My mother, Dorothy, performed some of her research about Father Durbin through Notre Dame University.

On page 15 of his book *The Catholic Church in Chicago*, Father James J. McGovern alludes to Father Badin as one who labored during the financial crisis of 1837 and beyond for the spiritual welfare of canal area Catholics. Unquestionably, Father Badin was in Chicago during 1846 working as chaplain to the Sisters of Mercy convent, and while working with the Sisters of Mercy, Father Baden became an inspiration to the children under the Sisters' instruction. He became resident pastor at Bourbonnais Grove, Illinois, near Kankakee, from 1846 until 1849. Father Badin was most likely not really a resident pastor, as the term is understood in the 20th century. Instead, it is probable that Father Badin had been visiting this mission ten years prior to this time. After all, the Bourbonnais mission had been a French-Canadian settlement of numerical strength for some time. It was one of the first missions served by Vincennes priests in the northern Illinois region.

"At the close of his career (Father) Badin was without a definite assignment and was permitted by Bishop Flaget to exercise his zeal wherever he found need." (Sister Mary Borromeo Brown, *History of the Sisters of Providence of Saint Mary of the Woods*, Vol. 1. New York, 1949, page 72). The good Father Badin died at Cincinnati on the 21st of April 1853, at 84 years of age. He had been demanding of others as the pioneer life had been demanding of him. In his lifetime he had been vicar general for Baltimore, Cincinnati, Bardstown, Vincennes and Chicago dioceses. His missionary career was legendary and would shape the thinking of all that tramped along the Holy Path in the United States.

As stated earlier, Reverend Stephen Badin was the first priest ordained in the United States. He had arrived in Kentucky from Baltimore in 1793 and directed Catholic life there until 1808, when the Diocese of Bardstown was erected with Reverend Benedict Flaget appointed as the first Bishop. After a great deal of resistance, Bishop John Carroll of Baltimore consecrated Flaget on November 4, 1810. Accompanied by recruits Simon Bruté, Guy Chabrat and John B. M. David, Flaget traveled to Bardstown and was installed on June 9, 1811. Before continuing with the structure of the early Catholic Church in Kentucky, the biography of Bishop Flaget should be examined. The following quoted material is from the Catholic Encyclopedia.

> Benedict Joseph Flaget was the first Bishop of Bardstown (subsequently of Louisville), Kentucky, U.S.A., b. at Contournat, near Billom, Auvergne, France, 7 November, 1763; d. 11 February, 1850, at Louisville, Kentucky. He was a posthumous child and was only two years old when his mother died, so an aunt cared for him and his brothers. They were welcomed at the home of their uncle, Canon Benoit

Flaget, at Billom. When he was seventeen years old, Flaget went to the Sulpician seminary of Clermont to study philosophy and theology. It was there that he joined the Society of St. Sulpice on November 1, 1783. He was ordained a priest in 1787, at Issy, where Father Gabriel Richard, the future apostle of Michigan, was then superior. Flaget taught dogmatic theology at Nantes for two years, and filled the same chair at the seminary of Angers when the French Revolution closed that house. He returned to Billom in 1791 and on the advice of the Sulpician superior, Father Emery, he became determined to devote himself to the American mission. He sailed in January 1792, with Father J. B. M. David, his future coadjutor, and the subdeacon Stephen Badin, landing in Baltimore March 29, 1792. He was studying English with his Sulpician brethren, when Bishop Carroll tested his self-sacrifice by sending him to Fort Vincennes, as missionary to the Indians and pastor of the Fort. Crossing the mountains he reached Pittsburg, where he had to lay over for six months because of low water in the Ohio River. He did such good work that he gained the lasting esteem of General Anthony Wayne. The latter recommended him to the military commander, Colonel Clark, at the Falls of the Ohio, who deemed it an honor to escort him to Fort Vincennes, where he arrived December 21, 1792. Father Flaget stayed there two years and then, recalled by his superiors, he became professor at the Georgetown College under the presidency of Father Dubourg. In November 1798, he was sent to Havana, from where he returned in 1801 with twenty-three students to Baltimore.

On 8 April, 1808, Bardstown, Kentucky, was created a see (a see refers to a bishop's town or his authority) and Flaget was named its first bishop. He refused the honour and his colleagues of St. Sulpice approved his action, but when in 1809 he went to Paris, his superior, Father Emery, received him with the greeting: "My Lord, you should be in your diocese! The pope commands you to accept." Leaving France with Father Simon William Bruté, the future Bishop of Vincennes, and the subdeacon, Guy Ignatius Chabrat, his future coadjutor in Kentucky. Flaget landed in Baltimore, and was consecrated 4 November 1810, by Archbishop Carroll. The Diocese of Bardstown comprised the whole Northwest, bounded east and west by Louisiana and the Mississippi. Bishop Flaget, handicapped by poverty, did not leave Baltimore until 11 May, 1811, and reached Louisville, 4 June, whence the Rev. C. Nerinckx escorted him to Bardstown. He arrived there 9 June. On Christmas of that year he ordained priest the Rev. Guy Ignatius Chabrat, the first priest ordained in the West. Before Easter, 1813, he had established priestly conferences, a seminary at St. Stephen's (removed to St. Thomas', November, 1811), and made two pastoral visits in Kentucky. That summer he visited the outlying districts of Indiana, Illinois, and Eastern Missouri, confirming 1,275 people during the trip.

Bishop Flaget's great experience, absolute self-denial, and holy life gave him great influence in the councils of the Church and at Rome. Most of the bishops appointed within the next twenty years were selected with his advice. In October, 1817, he went to St. Louis to prepare the way for Bishop Dubourg. He recommended Bishop Fenwick for Ohio, then left on a trip through that state, Indiana, and Michigan in 1818. In the latter State he did great missionary work at Detroit and Monroe, attending also a rally of 10,000 Indians at St. Mary's. Upon his return to Kentucky in 1819 he consecrated his new cathedral in Bardstown, 8 August, and consecrated therein his first coadjutor bishop, Rev. J. B. M. David, on the 15th. In 1821 he started on a visitation of Tennessee, and bought property in Nashville for the first Catholic church. The years 1819 to 1821 were devoted to missionary work among the Indians. He celebrated the first Synod of Bardstown, 8 August, 1823, and continued his labours until 1828, when he was called to Baltimore to consecrate Archbishop Whitfield; there he attended the first Council of Baltimore in 1829. In 1830 he consecrated one of his own priests, Rev. Richard Kenrick, as Bishop of Philadelphia. A great friend of education, he invited the Jesuits to take charge of St. Mary's College, Bardstown, in 1832. In the meantime he had resigned his see in favour of Bishop David with Bishop Chabrat as coadjutor. Both priests and people rebelled, and their representations were so instant and continued that Rome recalled its appointment and reinstated Bishop Flaget, who during all this time was, regardless of age and infirmities, attending the cholera-stricken in Louisville, Bardstown, and surrounding country during 1832 and 1833. Bishop Chabrat became his second coadjutor and was consecrated 20 July, 1834. Only Kentucky and Tennessee were now left under Flaget's jurisdiction, and in the former he founded various religious institutions, including four colleges, two convents, one foundation of brothers, and two religious institutions of priests. Tennessee became a diocese with see at Nashville in 1838.

His only visit to Europe and Rome was not undertaken until 1835. He spent four years in France and Italy in the interests of his diocese and of the propogation of the Faith, visiting forty-six dioceses. Everywhere he edified the people by the sanctity of his life, and well authenticated miracles are ascribed to his intercession. He returned to America in 1839, transferred his see to Louisville, and crowned his fruitful life by consecrating, 10 September, 1848, a young Kentucky priest, Martin John Spalding, as his third coadjutor and successor in the see of Louisville. The corner-stone of the cathedral of Louisville was laid 15 August, 1849. He died peacefully at Louisville, sincerely mourned and remembered to this day. His only writings are his journal and a report of his diocese to the Holy See.

Two orders of religious women, the Sisters of Loretto and the Sisters of Charity, were founded in 1812 and they staffed schools, orphanages, and hospitals. In 1823 the Dominican Sisters of St. Catherine were formed and the order grew large enough to staff hospitals, a college, and grade and high schools. These are only a few examples of the growing number of religious congregations in the diocese and the services they performed.

Bishop Flaget called the first diocesan synod in February 1812. At this time a dispute over Church lands began between Badin and Flaget. Flaget wanted Badin, who held title to practically all of the land through his own purchase, to turn all title over to him, with no conditions. Canon law was not clear on this matter, and the land in question was not legally settled until Badin made transfer in his last will and testament.

Flaget served as Bishop for forty years, and among his many accomplishments was the building of the St. Joseph's Cathedral in Bardstown in 1819; the first Cathedral west of the Alleghenies. In 1841 Flaget moved the see from Bardstown to Louisville after petitioning of Rome. In 1848 he consecrated Martin J.

Spalding coadjutor bishop, and in 1849 the cornerstone of the new Cathedral of the Assumption in Louisville was blessed. When Bishop Flaget died in February of 1850, Spalding became the second Bishop of Louisville.

Father Elisha John Durbin was ordained in 1822, but by this time the Civil War was consuming everybody's attention, especially Father Durbin's. He spent the war years attending to the souls of the Union and Confederate soldiers.

Under Spalding's leadership, institutions and parishes grew in number, although the United States Civil War caused much disruption. In June 1864, Spalding was transferred to the see of Baltimore. His brother and vicar-general, Benedict J. Spalding, served as administrator until Peter Joseph Lavialle was consecrated on September 24, 1865. Lavialle's tenure was not long because of his untimely death on May 11, 1867.

William George McCloskey, the rector of the American College in Rome, was appointed Bishop of Louisville to succeed Lavialle on March 3, 1868 and was consecrated in Rome on May 24, 1868. McCloskey's forty-one year episcopate was marred by many disputes with both institutions and religious orders, and as a result many left the diocese. Conversely, other orders came to the diocese, and McCloskey's tenure is considered one of Catholic advancement in the diocese.
(Sources for this historical sketch include: *Louisville, Archdiocese of*, by J. H. Schauinger, *New Catholic Encyclopedia*, McGraw-Hill Book Company: New York, Vol. VIII pages 1028-1031 and *An American Holy Land: A History of the Archdiocese of Louisville*, by Clyde F. Crews, Michael Glazier, Inc.: Wilmington, Delaware, 1987.)

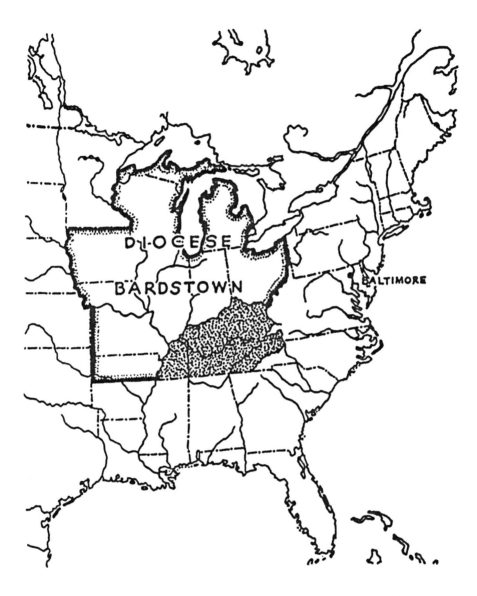

Diocese of Bardstown, Kentucky containing the parish served by
REVEREND FATHER ELISHA JOHN DURBIN (1800-1887)

Now, with the background of these devoted clerics having been studied, we proceed with the story of Father Durbin.

The parents of Patience Logsdon, Father Durbin's mother, were Elisha and Rebecca (Howard) Logsdon. Elisha was married twice and had at least fourteen children between his two wives. Elisha, also an early Kentucky settler, had four sons and ten daughters. Elisha's parents were William and Ann (Davis) Logsdon. This William was the brother of Ann Logsdon who married Samuel S. Durbin, and the latter were the parents of Christopher Durbin. This means that husband and wife, "Blind Johnny" and Patience, were also second cousins. Just about every Durbin in America can trace their ancestry back to Samuel Durbin and Ann (Logsdon) Durbin.

In civilized society incest is considered taboo. However, incest is more usually defined as prohibited heterosexual relations between siblings or between parents and their children. There are even laws against it. Some religions and some societies forbid marriages between cousins; however, a marriage between first cousins is not necessarily, by definition, incest. To marry a cousin back in those days was not unusual. In early American communities, which were few and far between, the people were acquainted with only a very few other people who were *not* their relatives.

This Christopher Durbin (1741-1825) married twice, first to Edith Margaret Logsdon, with whom he had five sons and one daughter. The parents of "Blind Johnny" Durbin, Reverend Durbin's father, were Christopher Durbin and his second wife, Margaret Brown Parkinson (her dates of birth and death are not known), with whom he had four sons. The place where Christopher and his family lived and died is well substantiated. Durbin family researchers, Mrs. Frank J. Stodden, Jr. (Lavern Stodden) and Mrs. Jan Bell Linn, list Christopher Durbin's place of death as Madison County, Kentucky. Furthermore, according to researcher Mrs. Evalou Gillock, Christopher Durbin is listed on the 1790 Tax List as living in Madison County, Kentucky, and in the 1800 census both he and Christopher Jr. were in Madison County. In reference to "Blind Johnny" Durbin, in 1800 John Durbin was listed as living in Madison County, Kentucky. This information was provided by Mrs. Dorothy Thomas Cullen of the Filson Club, located at 118 West Breckenridge Street in Louisville, Kentucky. (The Filson Club was organized May 15, 1884 for collecting, preserving and publishing historical material, especially that pertaining to Kentucky.) Christopher's oldest son, Edward Durbin, moved to Barren County, Kentucky. He was a "wagoner" hauling such supplies as salt and lumber. His only road was a creek bed and his pay consisted of pork and tobacco.

The following few paragraphs contain information Dorothy acquired from the *History of the Diocese of Covington, Kentucky, Eastern Kentucky—part of the*

Diocese of Quebec at the Kentucky Building, Western Kentucky University, Bowling Green, Kentucky on August 25, 1973.

> A sample study of the early Catholic pioneers to eastern Kentucky may be had in the case of the Durbin family which is considered to be the oldest Catholic family in the Covington Diocese today. Their descendants in present Lee and Estill counties have retained the Faith from pioneer days. The original Kentucky progenitor of all the Durbins found within Kentucky at present and of the many who have migrated in the course of the last century to the west and north was Christopher Durbin. He came from Maryland, where his Irish ancestors had lived since the early days of the Maryland colony. He came to Kentucky by way of North Carolina over the Wilderness Road, settling in Madison County. Traditions in that section of the Diocese, along with general deductions from the earliest available tax-book records of Madison County, would seem to point to 1779 or 1780 as the possible date for the coming of Christopher Durbin to Kentucky.

It should be noted here that there is actually only a small amount of Irish blood in the Durbin family line. They were mostly English.

According to the reference,

> Christopher Durbin had a family of twelve children, six sons and six daughters, most of whom were fully grown by the beginning of the nineteenth century. The lists in the tax-book would seem to indicate that the names of the sons were Edward, John, Joseph, Thomas, Austin and Nicholas. Many of the descendants of Christopher Durbin left eastern Kentucky along with other Catholic pioneers of Madison County who, deprived of religious advantages, sought new homes in one or the other Catholic settlements of the State or outside the State. The descendants of the early Durbins who remained in the territory of the present Diocese of Covington were mostly descendants of Edward ("Ned") Durbin, son of Christopher.

> Edward Durbin, his wife Betty (Porter) and family moved to Barren County, Kentucky. By trade he was a "wagoner." He hauled supplies such as salt, lumber, and metals from one comrnunity to another, the creek-beds being his roads.

Edward Durbin had a large family, but the names of only the following children are now known—Kit, Sam, Ned, Susan, Philip, John and Joe.

Of Kit, Sam and Ned Durbin, little is now known beyond their names. When business brought Edward Durbin through Madison County he was accustomed to stay overnight at the home of Edward Logsden (Logsdon), one of the pioneer families of Madison County. Two of the children of Edward Durbin married into the Logsden family, Joseph Durbin marrying Edith Logsden, and Susan Durbin marrying John Logsden. Philip Durbin made his home in Madison County, settling on Drowning Creek. Missionaries, probably as late as the 1830's, offered Mass in his humble home. When Father Kenrick was pastor of White Sulphur (1827), he said Mass in the home of Philip Durbin on Drowning Creek. Philip was regarded as a famous controversialist. Of his family no trace remains today. The immediate ancestors of all the Durbins in the Diocese today were the two sons of Edward, John and Joe, who settled in Lee County. John Durbin married Nancy Ann Wagers, of the Catholic Wagers family, which at the beginning of the nineteenth century, had settled at Station Camp on Red River in Estill County.

John and Joe Durbin moved from Madison County into Lee County about 1815; both were married at the time, John being the older. Joe built his first log cabin home on the banks of the Kentucky River, about half a mile from Old Landing. John went farther up the river, six or eight miles, to what is now Yellow Rock.

Joe Durbin and his wife, Edith Logsden, had a large family, at least ten children whose names are known, five boys and five girls. His wife, Edith, died in 1867, and he afterwards married the widow of Jim Carter nee Cynthia Wiatt. By this union, there were two children, Mary and Bill, neither of whom was baptized Catholic. Joe Durbin subsequently bought a tract of land on Contrary Creek, Lee County, where he erected a cabin. He died April 15, 1877.

The marriage of John Durbin and Nancy Ann Wagers was blessed with thirteen children, nine boys and four girls. John

Durbin's first wife, Nancy Ann Wagers Durbin, died when the children were very young. He married again, his second wife being Julia Mahan (Mann). This union also was blessed with thirteen children, five of whom died in infancy or early childhood. John Durbin lived with his family at various places along the river in the vicinity of Yellow Rock. He also later settled on Contrary Creek, below the Middle Fork, where he survived his brother, Joe, some years. His remains were buried at White Ash. Marion, Haid, Pius, and Joe, sons of John Durbin, were instrumental in erecting a Catholic church on their land at Station Camp, which remained a mission center in Estill County, bearing the name of St. Paul Mission, until it was sold by the Diocese in 1912.

Most of the Durbin descendants who have retained the Faith in the Diocese are descendants of John Durbin. The posterity of Joe Durbin, who continued to reside in the present territory of the Diocese, are for the most part, no longer of the Faith. A strain of the Durbins at Belle Pointe, Contrary Creek, Lee County, remained loyal to the Faith; such of them as the families of Jim Durbin, Lucien Durbin, and Jim Blaine Durbin, were descendants of both John and Joe through the intermarriage of their children, Rill and Joe, first cousins. During the period in which the St. Theresa Mission Center school on Contrary Creek flourished, under the guidance of Bishop Howard, there were children at the school who were the great-great-great-great grandchildren of Christopher Durbin, removed from him by seven generations. The Durbins in Lee and Estill counties today, who attend Church as regular communicants, in general, trace their lineage back to John Durbin, son of Edward Durbin, son of Christopher. They stand today as the descendants of a pioneer Catholic family which settled in frontier Kentucky.

The preservation of the Faith in the Durbin family, especially by the earlier generations, was by a special blessing of God. In the case of some of them, personal contact with a priest was a privilege afforded to them about twice in the course of a normal life time. Father Henry B. Schulte in his study of the Kentucky Durbins relates the following personal experience:

> On the occasion of my first contact with Aunt Mymie,...[youngest child of Joe Durbin and Edith Logsden], she contended that she had not been to the sacraments nor had she seen a priest for 75 years. My immediate reaction to that contention was that the old lady was drawing the long bow to a long limit; but on filling in inter-related dates and occurrences of her life and comparing them with others which I had before established, the conviction was forced on me that the contention in point was timed to a twelvemonth. It should be put down, though, that the fact that Aunt Mymie escaped, during the last 25 years, the searching eyes of priests, who during that time conscientiously herded a widely-scattered flock, is in the nature of an accident. But the fifty years previous were no accident.

The slow development of the Church in this section of the State forced such conditions upon the scattered Catholics. From the time of the earliest missionaries to Kentucky until long after the Diocese was formed, when Richmond received a resident pastor and a band of missionaries in 1906, there was no resident priest in this immediate vicinity. The visits of the missionaries were irregular and often at long intervals. The Catholic families of the section were scattered along the creeks. To a great extent, the Catholics here, as elsewhere in similar regions, were left to preserve the Faith in whatever way possible. The preservation of the Faith depended much on the zeal of individuals. Nor was lay leadership lacking in the southern section of the present Diocese of Covington. The early pioneer Catholics in Madison County were staunch Catholics honesty stamping their rugged way of living. Christopher Durbin became the recognized leader in Catholic activities. He was often known to ride to St. Stephen's, the residence of Father Badin, a distance of eighty miles, where he took young couples in order that a.... (The remainder of the quoted material is not available, but it probably said, in effect, that Christopher took young couples to St. Stephen's so they could be married by a Catholic priest.)

According to Equity Court Dockets of Allegany County, Maryland, in 1796 Bennett Logsdon accused Christopher and Edward Durbin of selling whiskey. A year later, to the month, they were acquitted. James Virden, a Durbin family researcher who corresponded with Dorothy, claims this does not make sense because Christopher was in Kentucky on the tax records during those years. He says Christopher went to Kentucky in 1779, but there is nothing to indicate he did not return to Maryland for a visit. Mr. Virden also has records of three boys claiming they were sons of Christopher, who applied for a guardian in the Orphans Court Records in the years 1825-1828. (Possibly the three boys were sons of Christopher, Jr.) B. J. Webb, author of *The Centenary of Catholicity in Kentucky*, mentioned the early settlements in Kentucky and said Christopher Durbin had six sons and six daughters. (Again, maybe this could be Christopher, Jr. instead.) Steve Barr, the Durbin family researcher, was going through law records in Madison County, Kentucky and came across a law suit over the Christopher Durbin estate, dated 1825, which carried through a couple of years.

(According to Carol Ann [Durbin] McKellar, who corresponded with Dorothy and this author, the Chief of Police in Flint, Michigan during the 1980s, Max Durbin, is Christopher Durbin's great-great-great grandson. Max Durbin has a brother, Robert Ross Durbin, now deceased, in St. Louis, Missouri. Robert's middle name just happens to be the same as Donald Ross Durbin, husband of Dorothy, and Donald was born in St. Louis.) Ross Durbin published *A Durbin Heritage* in November 2000, and it consists of 189 spiral-bound pages containing a wealth of information on the Durbin families, especially those in Kentucky. I have formal permission to use some of his material. After a long illness, Robert passed away on January 10, 2001, but he had the good fortune to see his book completed before his passing.

From the Hall of Records, Annapolis, Maryland, which Dorothy visited in 1965, under "Oaths of Fidelity" is listed "CHRISTOPHER Durbin 1778 Baltimore." Christopher served in the Revolutionary War.

Dorothy's notes say that some of these records presumably were taken from a book in the Greene County, Pennsylvania Library by a Durbin researcher. More information on Christopher and his descendants came from W. Jesse Durbin who said he received from Mrs. Gillock a copy of the records of administration of Christopher Durbin deceased December 29, 1825 on motion of Christopher K. Durbin in which the following or any three of them ordered to report to the said court—Edward L. Shackelford, Richard Apperson, Henry B. Hawkins and Willard Goodloe. (These four just named were probably sons-in-law of Christopher Durbin, deceased.)

Christopher Durbin was the eleventh of the thirteen children of Samuel S. Durbin and Ann Logsdon. Most Durbins in America today can trace their ancestry back to Samuel and Ann in Maryland. Samuel's will was probated in 1752, in Frederick County, Maryland, Liber 28, Folio 400 (Land Office, Annapolis, Maryland, 1634-1777). This will was also executed in Frederick County, Liber 65-10-6, 11 May 1753. Some of the information on Samuel S. Durbin came from St. Paul's Parish, Baltimore Register Volume 1 1710-1808, Maryland Historical Society, which Dorothy visited in May 1965. From this information, his children's birth dates were verified.

From the Hall of Records, Annapolis, Maryland, visited in 1965, under "Testamentary Proceedings" is listed "SAMUEL DURBIN 1752, 1753, 1754, 1776, Frederick." The Maryland Calendar of Wills, Volume VI, 1727, page 39, William Holland of Baltimore County named Thomas Durbin (Samuel's father), personalty (personal property). Samuel Durbin was named Testator.

This will, copied from the Hall of Records, Annapolis, Maryland in May 1965, makes for interesting reading today:

> 1752 SAMUEL S. DURBIN, Planter—Will September 19, 1752, Frederick County:
>
> To son WILLIAM, 100 Acres Cobb's Choice to take said land at lower end and not take any improvements of my dwelling plantation. To daughter ANN, 1 cow and calf. To daughter MARGARET, 1 heifer yearling. To son THOMAS, 1 heifer yearling. To son JOHN, sorrel mares cold. Christopher to son-in-law Canon 1 horse and wagon, daughter-in-law 1 cow and calf. Dear and loving wife (exec.) keep all above 'till her death if she don't marry. Dwelling and plantation to well-beloved son SAMUEL, 50 acres with all appurtenances—remainder divided among remaining children.
>
> Wit: THOMAS LOGSDON, Wm. Wilson, Testator: Samuel

From Frederick County, Maryland Courthouse, Deeds, General Index, May 1965, comes the following:

> (WILLIAM SR. DIED—SAMUEL REQUESTED) At request of Samuel S. Durbin, farmer, the following release was recorded 25 August 1769: William Durbin of Little Pipe Creek hundred in Frederick County—whereas Samuel Durbin, late of Pipe Creek aforesaid deceased father of William Durbin, Cobb's Choice and to his son Samuel Durbin, Jr. After decease of Ann Durbin (wife) Wit: John Logsdon, George Mathews.

(The "hundred" in the Little Pipe Creek hundred just mentioned, can probably best be described as the predecessor of the county of today. There were many of these "hundreds." Maryland was later divided into counties, and even later these early counties were again divided into more counties. These changes made family research somewhat difficult.)

The house of Samuel Durbin and Ann (Logsdon) Durbin was built in 1741. (There is the date of 1767 on the side of the house.) The following was written by Mr. Howard Steiner of Harrisburg, Pennsylvania:

> This is a wonderful home, still standing, in good condition and has been made a shrine by the Methodist Church of America. There are roadside signs pointing to its location about two miles out from Westminster, Maryland. The Durbins became interested in Methodism (Samuel's son, William, became a Methodist in 1768) and the first American ordained bishop, Francis Asbury (1745-1816) often visited with the Durbins during three generations of that family, preached in their home as well as Robert Strawbridge, recognized by many as the first Methodist preacher in America. He was a near neighbor and friend. The Durbins were active in establishing Methodism in this country and William belonged to the First Society of Methodism.

Part of the home is now used as a golf club facility with adjacent greens. There is speculation that the older building near this home was the log cabin Samuel built, where son Christopher was born.

Samuel and Ann were married in St. Paul's Church, in Baltimore, Maryland. Dorothy had a newspaper clipping, date unknown, which may be of interest:

> Church Looks Back, BALTIMORE, Md. (AP)—Old St. Paul's Church has launched a year-long celebration of its 275th anniversary with services which resembled those of a Sunday morning in 1692, the year the Episcopal parish was founded. The Rev. Halsey M. Cook, rector, wore a powdered wig and asked God's blessing upon 'our monarchs, William and Mary.' The ushers wore plumed hats, velvet and lace.

Dorothy also had part of what appeared to be a magazine clipping that reads, "DESIDERATA PLAQUE is a collection of principles to live by. Found in Old Saint Paul's Church in Baltimore and dated 1692, the advice seems just as suitable today as to that long-ago time. Fully laminated on wood plaque,...."

Dorothy had also typed this note, which may have something to do with Old St. Paul's:

> St. Inigoes Neck, city of St. Mary's (oldest in Md.) in 1639 to Jesuit priest 'Mr.' Ferdinand POULTON Chapel Lot, first English Roman Catholic Church in this country.

Samuel Durbin was the apparent overseer of roads, including "Old Garrison Road" near Owings Mills and Pikeville in Maryland.

For over 100 years, Durbins intermarried with Logsdons. Durbins and Logsdons were numerous in Frederick County, Maryland, and later they moved west, settling near Fort Cumberland and Mount Savage. They jumped the state line north of Mount Savage and lived in Fayette, Somerset and Bedford Counties in Pennsylvania. By 1800 all had left Maryland. In a letter from Edward Ewing Adams to Edwin C. Welch, a noted researcher and author, 23 November 1943:

> Durbin families intermarried so it would take more than the proverbial Philadelphia lawyer to unravel the tangled skeins. It would take some of the brightest braintrusters down in Washington.

(Mr. Welch corresponded with Dorothy's husband Donald between 1944 and 1949. Mr. Welch also provided much information to W. Jesse Durbin and other Durbin family researchers.)

In a letter from W. Jesse Durbin to Mr. Welch December 1, 1943: "Our generation in Illinois spent money more than once investigating the 'fabulous estates in Baltimore'." And in a letter from Mr. Welch to W. Jesse Durbin, 11 December 1943:

> This work, which someone in some future generation will thank us for, is valuable only to posterity and as such should be preserved. To trace one family, you must trace the other (Durbin—Logsdon). There is a gap between 1750 and 1800, almost a blank. Durbins and Logsdons didn't *push* the frontier of this country back, they *pulled* them back—hence all records are probably made by circuit riding parsons and inevitably lost.

According to Scharff, author of *History of Western Maryland*, in 1742 about 200 parishioners petitioned the Governor and Assembly for a preacher. No Logsdon or Durbin names were on that petition, but in 1758 about 250 "freeholders and freemen" made another petition. Some of the names: THOMAS

LAYDON, JAMES LOGUE, JOHN FOWLER, GEORGE BROWN JR., SAMUEL ELLIS, JAMES ELLIS, ZACHARIS ELLIS, THOMAS DURBIN, JOHN DURBIN, SAMUEL DURBIN, and WILLIAM DURBIN.

In 1762, in the Middleburg District of Carroll County, Maryland, NORMAN BRUCE and FRANCIS SCOTT KEY, who wrote our National Anthem, are listed as pioneer settlers. (Some or all of the Durbins undoubtedly were their neighbors and probably knew them well.) Also listed are New Windsor District pioneers JAMES CARROLL who owned the 2,680-acre "Park Hall," HENRY WILLIS, RICHARD STEVENSON, POULSONS, and DURBINS. (For reasons unknown, Dorothy noted that Ann Poulson died 21 December 1875 at age 78.) Also in 1762, in the Middleburg District: DANIEL McKINZEY, 5,301-acre "New Bedford," and JOHN LOGSDON. In 1741 "Fanneys Meadow" to JAMES WALLS, FRANCIS SCOTT KEY "Terra Rubram," and COL. JOSHUA GIST. In 1789 LAWRENCE LOGSDON and JOSHUA GIST were owners of a vast "adj." (adjunct?). "Friendship Completed" was owned by JNO. FOWLER and WILLIAM HAYDEN (in section WG-DD 441). LAWRENCE LOGSDON bought 100 acres bounding on "Friendship Completed" in 1794 from JNO. FOWLER and HANNAH, his wife (in section WG-NN 344).

Samuel Durbin and Francis Scott Key were obviously neighbors and probably were friends. To digress from this story of Father Elisha John Durbin's background, it's unlikely that Francis Scott Key thought he was writing the future national anthem when, during the War of 1812, he composed the *Star Spangled Banner*. The words were written in September of 1814 when Key witnessed the British shelling of Fort McHenry in Baltimore harbor. After an anxious night during which the fate of the fort was in doubt, Key was deeply moved when "by the dawn's early light" he saw that "our flag was still there." He set his poem to the tune *To Anacreon In Heaven*. Anacreon was a Fifth Century BC Greek poet whose lyrics in praise of love and wine were the stimulus for the founding of the Anacreonic Society, an Eighteenth Century group of British bon vivants. The music of *To Anacreon In Heaven* was composed by one of the members of the society, probably John Stafford Smith. It was first printed in 1799 and soon became well known in America. No less than 85 different lyrics were set to the tune including an earlier one by Francis Scott Key himself. By late 1814 *The Star Spangled Banner* (Key's original title was *Defence of Fort McHenry*) was being sung throughout the States, and although it did not become our national anthem until 1931, it was always considered the preeminent American song. (This information was found on page 5 of the Music Workshop section on the March/April 1995 issue of *Sheet Music Magazine*.)

As for Christopher's mother, Ann Logsdon, her name was misspelled *LOGDEN* in St. Paul's Parish, Baltimore Register Volume 1, 1710-1808, Maryland Historical Society, May 1965 (from which some of the following information came). Steve Barr recorded her year of death as 1770, Frederick County, Maryland, but there appears to be no proof of this.

September 19, 1729, William Logsdon deeded to his "beloved daughter Ann Durbin," the one hundred acre tract called "Pleasant Green" on the north side of Maryland's Potapsco River, and it included "houses, outhouses, barns, stables, tobacco sheds, orchards, fences, etc." This tract lay between the branches of Great Pipe Creek and Little Pipe Creek in Carroll County, just west of Westminster. (Incidentally, records of Durbin families up to 1836 are in Frederick County, Maryland according to Mr. E. C. Welch.)

In the Maryland Calendar of Wills, Volume VII, 1735, pages 169-189, Theophilus Jones, Baltimore County, St. John's Parish, Ann Durbin was Testator. From the Hall of Records, Annapolis, Maryland, visited in 1965, in the "Testamentary Proceedings" is listed "ANN Durbin 1754 Frederick County 1777 Harford County."

Dorothy copied from the Hall of Records in Annapolis, Maryland, in May 1965: "Accounts. Liber 36, Folio 505; 1753 Wills L38, F134 & 137; 1770 Wills Bx 4, F52; L54 F115, 11 May 1753," Ann is listed as Executrix of her husband Samuel's will.

ANN Durbin (Widow of Samuel S. Durbin)—Will July 8, 1770

Sons WILLIAM, SAMUEL, THOMAS, JOHN, NICHOLAS, CHRISTOPHER

To each at end of one year 1 shilling sterling and no more of estate. To son EDWARD one black mare branded thus ___ and no more. To son BENJAMIN 1 feather bed and furniture and one large iron pot and no more. To four daughters, SARAH McKENSEY, ANN STEVENSON, MARGARET BROWN and MARY LOGSDON 1 shilling sterling and no more. To HONOUR 2 cows and calves and one feather bed and furniture and all household.

Son EDWARD Exec. Wit: JOHN LOGSDON, WILLIAM LOGSDON

To complete the investigation into Father Durbin's roots, we should also include the parents of Samuel Durbin and Ann Logsdon. Thomas Durbin (born before 1680, died in 1699; Dorothy referred to him as "Thomas III") was the father of Samuel S. Durbin, and he is mentioned in the will of his father, the Thomas Durbin (born sometime before 1655 and died sometime before 1720) who came to America in 1663. Dorothy had a hunch that Samuel S. Durbin was a brother of John Durbin Sr., and thus a son of Thomas Durbin III. We will leave it like that until something proves otherwise.

A legend in Luella Frye's family is that this Thomas was Catholic and his wife was Methodist and that they had four sons, two of whom became priests, and the other two became Methodist preachers. Son John was Methodist and son Samuel was Catholic, but none actually became priests as far as anyone knows. (Luella Frye was a Durbin researcher who lived in Mount Vernon, Ohio. She corresponded with Dorothy in the early 1960s.)

In the Maryland Calendar of Wills, Volume VI, 1727, page 39, William Holland of Baltimore County named Thomas Durbin, personalty. Samuel Durbin was named Testator. In Volume VII, 1735, pages 169-189, Robert Robinson of Baltimore County, 1736, named Thomas Durbin as Testator. He is also in the records kept by Mary W. Durbin, Rt. #1, Bellville, Ohio 44813. Also see the Durbin family in the *History of Union County*, Kentucky, 1886, page 317. This document was found at the DAR (Daughters of the American Revolution) Library, Washington, DC, which Dorothy visited in November 1964.

All that is known about Thomas' wife is that she was a daughter of John Downs (birth date unknown; died in 1718). In the Maryland Calendar of Wills, Volume IV, is listed a will of Downs, John, planter, Baltimore County April 1, 1718, June 3, 1718. It reads, "To Rose Trotten and heirs 1/3 estate and personalty; to son-in-law Simon Cannon and daughter-in-law Elizabeth Cannon, personalty, to be of age at decease of testator; to sons-in-law Thomas and Christopher Durbin, personalty, to be of age at 18 years." Thomas' brother,

Christopher, also married a daughter of John Downs. (A John Downs was listed as a soldier for 3 years in the Continental Line Warrants District of Ohio Infantry, Bounty Land Warrants, Revolutionary War Records, Volume 1, Virginia, by Brumbaugh.)

The last person to be named in the ancestry of Father Durbin is the father of the aforementioned Thomas Durbin. He is the Thomas Durbin (born before 1655 and died before 1720; wife not known) who sailed from Bristol, England in 1663. His will is dated 1699, and Dorothy was able to estimate his birth date from information therein. His will mentions sons Christopher (1684-1709), William and the previously mentioned Thomas. According to *Maryland Records*, Volume II, by Brumbaugh, the Testator of his will was Jane Long, June 3, 1696. From the Hall of Records, Annapolis, Maryland (which Dorothy visited in May 1965), his will inventory, 1699, "late of Baltimore County" lists "funeral charges of Thomas and wife" and "2 black walnut coffins."

The first reference to a Durbin in America is on page 91 in R. S. Glover's *Bristol and America*. Thomas Durbin sailed from Bristol, England (1654-1663), destination "Nevis." (Nevis probably refers to Saint Kitts-Nevis-Anguilla in the West Indies. On page 787, The New Encyclopaedia Britannica's Micropaedia, Volume VIII, 15th Edition, it is officially Saint Christopher-Nevis-Anguilla, three islands in the east Caribbean Sea politically linked and associated with Great Britain. The name Nevis derives from Christopher Columbus' likening the cloud-topped Nevis Peak to las nieves, or "the snows," when he discovered the island in 1493. It was settled by the English in 1628. Charlestown is the chief town and port.) Page 136, *Bristol and America* references a William Durbin, ship "Nevis Adventure" and a John Durbin who sailed to Barbados in 1663. According to this book, these people came to America from all parts of the British Isles and from all classes. In the *History of Somerset*, some of the Durbins were from Somersetshire, England.

According to family stories, two Durbin brothers came over from England in the time of Lord Baltimore in the middle 1600s, arriving in Maryland. Thomas was the first documented Durbin, mentioned in 1676. The other brother was probably the above-mentioned William or John. It was more likely that John was the brother because he arrived the same year as Thomas and the above William Durbin could possibly have been John's son. Many, if not most of the ships sailing from England to America first stopped at any of several Caribbean islands. John and his wife Mary (Drax) stopped in Barbados, and I was able to verify that John and Mary spent some time there. I visited the Barbados archives in 1998 and found John and Mary listed in Volume XV of *Servants to Foreign Plantations From Bristol, England, to Barbados, 1654-1686*. The Drax name also figured prominently in Barbados. The Drax family owned a large sugar plantation there and Drax Hall was built in the 1650s and is still standing in the town of St. George.

Dorothy had found references about Lord Baltimore and the Catholic settlers in Maryland. The following information was found in the Maryland Archives, Calvert Papers, Calendar State Papers, Colonial 1574-1660, Maryland Magazine (Battle Creek, Michigan Library).

The family of Lord Baltimore's mother was Catholic, and he wanted to find a refuge for his Roman Catholic brethren. Maryland, especially the area known as Arundel, became his choice. Maryland was named in honor of the Queen of England. Vessels departed for America between June 20, 1632 and August 20, 1633. Jesuit fathers sponsored the undertaking and received much publicity. Selection of applicants proceeded rapidly. Lord Baltimore issued many clear-cut statements that were needed to draw the rank and file to his cause. The number of applicants was never very large, but many Roman Catholic gentlemen and servants were already committed to the undertaking and probably shared in the expense. Two of the ships, the "Ark" and "Dove", became known as the Catholic transportation to the New World. Catholic priests and laymen either hid or boarded the ships secretly to avoid taking the oath denying papal authority in England (required by the proclamation of 1611). They arrived in the Capes of Virginia February 27, 1634. At that time, between 200 and 300 people landed on Maryland soil. Lord Baltimore died in Ireland at 52, and his son Cecelius 26, was chartered as the new Lord Baltimore June 30, 1632. Cecelius, Lord Baltimore, was also expected to go but he could not leave because affairs in England precluded it. Governorship of the colony passed to their brother Leonard, captain of the ship "St. Claude". Leonard died in 1647.

Here is an interesting anecdote. The first Lord Baltimore, who established the city of Baltimore, was an ardent shell collector, having one of the great collections of the world. The collection descended to his line until World War II when it was sent to New York and auctioned.

Due to much suspicion and mistrust, the Ark (Captain Robert Wintour, Commander) and Dove were delayed several months before sailing from London to Cowes, and several weeks in the harbor of Cowes on the Isle of Wight in England before heading for "Merrie Land." Not many bid farewell, and left family and sweethearts in London. On the Ark and the Dove were 17 gentlemen adventurers and their ladies, 2 priests and 200 commoners. "Beere delivered to ship Arke (several grades), 12 pipes of Canary wine." On St. Clements Island women landed for washing and some nearly drowned when a boat capsized. Their linens were lost. Only two women proved definitely to be aboard (there was no record of wives with husbands). On Blakiston Island in the Potomac River a lonely cross marks the landing "humbly recited on bended knees Litanies of the Sacred Heart with great emotion." On the mainland they immediately made friends with the Indians and founded the community of St. "Marries" (St. Mary's was named in honor of the Blessed Virgin Mary and was established on the feast of the Annunciation, March 25, 1634 at St. Clement's Island in the Potomac), and from this settlement they spread north and across the bay to the eastern shore. Maryland settlers turned wilderness into estates with names like "Penny Come Quick, My Lord's Gift, Truth's Fortune, I Have Been a Great While At (also known as the 'Cow Pasture')."

The Catholic Encyclopedia at the Battle Creek, Michigan Library indicates that the Diocese of Baltimore, founded April 6, 1789 was primarily composed of English, Irish, and German immigrants. The first colony landed March 25, 1634 under Leonard Calvert's leadership. The first three Lord Baltimores, George, Cecilius, and Charles were Catholic. Reverend Benedict Neale was the priest at Priest's Ford, Harford County in 1747. According to the Georgetown University Jesuits in 1791, during the Revolutionary War Maryland's best Catholic names were on the rolls of the Continental Army.

On page 29 of *American Irish*, by Shannon, it is said that most of the important Irish Catholics in the Colonial period were CARROLLS, the first of whom came to Maryland in 1688, under patronage of the Catholic King James II. Charles Carroll of Carrolton was born in 1737 and lived to age 95. He was the only Catholic, the wealthiest, and the longest-lived of the signers of the Declaration of Independence. Daniel Carroll, Charles' cousin, was a delegate to the Constitutional Convention. John Carroll, also a cousin, became the first Catholic Bishop in the United States.

In a narrative about George Pius Durbin, founder of the community of Durbin, Ohio, "The American progenitor of the Durbin family came to this country with the colony brought over by Lord Baltimore, in 1638, and settled on the spot where each of the ancestors of the subject, in a direct line, was born and reared." (See page 268, *Van Wert and Mercer Counties 1896 Biographical History*.) The town of Durbin, Ohio is no longer shown on maps of the area, but the main crossroads and some of the original buildings remain.

From *The Maryland and Delaware Genealogist*, Vol. 3, p. 67, 1962, DAR Library, Washington, DC, which Dorothy visited in November 1964, the first documented Durbin found in Maryland is noted in *Maryland Historical Magazine*, Vol. 39, p. 274.

> October 13, 1676 Walter Dickenson, Planter of Great Choptank, Talbot County, Maryland for 2,500 pounds tobacco, conveys to THOMAS DURBIN of Severne, Anne Arundel

> County the 200 acre tract 'Johnson' on east side of Dickenson Branch on east side of Welchman's Creek on the north side of the Potapscoe River.

Tract "Johnson" was patented to John Dickenson February 3, 1659 or 1660 and assigned by him to Walter Dickenson. THOMAS DURBIN was witness on two early deeds July 1, 1679, for Christopher Tapley; June 14, 1682, for Christopher Gist; a witness to the 1692 will of Jane Long. (Dorothy assumed Thomas Durbin settled in Severn prior to 1676 and that he was born prior to 1655, moved to Baltimore County after 1676 and died prior to 1720.)

In the *Maryland Genealogical Notes* by Wilkins, which Dorothy found in the State Library, Lansing, Michigan is listed:

> THOMAS DURBIN—Taxables taken of the Northside of Patapscoe hundred—1692, 1 Taxable—1694, 1 Taxable—1695, 1 Taxable.

Mr. Lawrence Hyter, another Durbin researcher who corresponded with Dorothy, found in the Baltimore Tax Records, July 1694-1695: "Potapsco hundred—south side of back river. North side of Potapsco Thomas Durbin—I." (Note that Potapsco is spelled "Patapsco" in the Encyclopaedia Britannica and on maps.) The estate called "Hab-Nab-At-A-Venture" was surveyed June 30, 1688 for orphans of Thomas Durbin. Humorously, "orphans" was spelled "orphants."

The following from *Life in Stuart England* by Maurice Ashley (not quoted directly) may be pertinent here. It describes conditions in England:

> Value of money in middle of 17th century was 15 to 20 times what it is today (author). Bristol, 2nd city in country, large city of great trade, streets very narrow. Stuart, England, from enthronement of James I in 1603 to death of Queen Anne in 1714. Many children—few survived—ordinary people couldn't afford doctors or midwives—disease or malnutrition. Ordinary men and women didn't marry very young, 26 for men, 22 for women, then lucky if had more than 10 years of life together. Not uncommon for village lads to get maidens into trouble. Breakfast—bread and beer at half past six. Bread made from rye, not wheat, not much cooking done in cottages, potatoes still unheard of. Ale, penny a quart. No tea and coffee, milk for children and invalids, cheese, ale and bread staples.

Women—3 gowns, 5 petticoat skirts, "safeguard" or apron, cloak, 2 hats, 3 waistcoats and "wearing linen and other necessities."

Men—doublet, hat, pair of leather breeches, pair of woolen breeches, a jerkin (a sleeveless jacket), 2 shirts, 4 bands, 2 pairs of shoes, total value 10 shillings.

Cottages—flimsy huts built of clay and branches of trees, without chimney or outlet for smoke except thru door. Windows rare, glass expensive. One or 2 rooms with loft or attic. Main room called hall, bedroom called chamber, sometimes divided in two. Might be kitchen and outhouse or buttery. An Act of 1589 forbade more than one family in each hut; some evidence exists that cottagers could not or would not find room to house their ageing parents.

Furniture—long oaken dining table with stools or benches, chairs rare, chests for storing, cheap, collapsible 'trundle' beds with feather or flock mattresses, food eaten off pewter plates with wooden spoons. Kettle or cauldron for cooking, logs for fuel (or cow dung or furze [a spiny yellow-flowered evergreen European shrub] used), light from rushlights (pith of a rush dipped in grease) or candles. Sanitary arrangements primitive.

To recount these relationships, the Thomas Durbin who came here from England, wife not known, had at least two sons, Christopher and Thomas. This second Thomas who married a daughter of John Downs, had Samuel S. Durbin who married Ann Logsdon. (Ann Logsdon was the daughter of the immigrant William Logsdon and Honor O'Flynn, both from Ireland.)

Samuel and Ann had thirteen children, the eleventh of whom was Christopher who became an early pioneer settler in Kentucky. (This author descended from Samuel's son Thomas; not Christopher.) Christopher married Margaret Brown Parkinson and they became the parents of John J. "Blind Johnny" Durbin who married Patience Logsdon. They, in turn, were the parents of the Reverend Father Elisha John Durbin.

Now we should take a look at Ann Logsdon's side of the family because that family's hardiness helps to show where Father Durbin inherited his endurance and strength. The Logsdons hail from strong human stock, and "Big Joe" Logsdon was one of our Nation's early "super-heroes."

Chapter 2

▼

Big Joe

Samuel's wife and Christopher's mother, Ann Logsdon, was the daughter of the immigrant, William Logsdon, who married Honor O'Flynn about 1702. Honor came to America from Ireland, where, it is told, she was kidnapped and brought here against her will. (According to a map from Irish International Airlines, families of the surname "O'Flynn" came from the area of Belfast, Antrim County, Northern Ireland.) It states in a letter from Mr. Welch to W. Jesse Durbin, that William Logsdon arrived in Maryland in 1683, an indentured man who served four years as such. William was an eager young man, and when he heard of the just-arrived ship carrying eligible young women, he secured the Captain's permission to board so that he might select a bride. As legend goes, William's eyes caught sight of the beautiful and young Honor O'Flynn, and love was suddenly and certainly in the air.

> Father Durbin comes of ancestry long noted for robust physical development and hardiness—his food and drink was simple. The Logsdons of Kentucky (recall, his mother was Patience Logsdon) were of large stature but Father Durbin's weight was not over 160 lbs., 5 feet 10 inches tall. In his younger days he had the appearance of a man of much nervous force and powers of endurance, rather than the appearance of an athlete. His face was somewhat tawny; it had not yet assumed the erysipelas (reddish) hue contracted from

constant exposure that marked his features for more than 40 years. He was quietly companionable and known to jest. He had wit and humor. (See the Durbin family on page 317, *History of Union County, Kentucky, 1886*.)

To illustrate the Logsdon traits for "robust physical development and hardiness," we must look at the life of "Big Joe" Logsdon, also called "Bulger Joe" (look at that word again; he did *not* play the bugle.). He was Father Elisha John Durbin's first cousin (two generations removed).

As this part of the story unfolds, keep in mind the threat that the Indians posed to the white settlers of America in those early days. There were Mohawk, Mohican, Oneida, Onondaga, Cayuga, Seneca, Iroquois, Susquehanna and many other Indian tribes throughout northeastern America until the white settlers displaced them, pushing the tribes ever westward. After moving from Maryland to Kentucky, Joseph would learn that the tribes to be feared in Kentucky were the Shawnee in the north and the Cherokee in the south. They were just as much of a threat to each other as they were to the white settlers. "Big Joe" Logsdon was there in the thick of things.

Joseph Logsdon was a personal friend of President George Washington. He is mentioned frequently in *George Washington's Diaries (1749-1799)*, Volume II, 1771-1785, pages 309-312 (regarding 1784 surveys in the vicinity of Back Bone Mountain, Garrett County, Maryland). George Washington was a surveyor, and according to the *Diaries*, Washington relied heavily on Joseph Logsdon and his father, Thomas Logsdon, because they knew the territory there better than anyone else. Joseph Logsdon's pastime was hunting.

Joseph and his wife, Susan, moved from Maryland to Kentucky and eventually to Illinois.

According to Collins' *History of Kentucky*, Joseph Logsdon was called into service by General Charles Scott as a scout to defend the borders of Madison County, Kentucky from May 1, 1792 to August 22, 1792.

Daniel Boone, whom we'll study in another chapter of this book, was supposed to have said, "Kaintucky is the cream of the world, with wild honey throwed in for good measure." Some of the early settlers came seeking land, while others came for freedom—freedom to expand. They were reckless, often lawless, and brave. One person who fit all these descriptions was "Big Joe" Logsdon. On pages 329-331 in Collins' *Historical Sketches of Kentucky*,

> About the year 1790, an individual known as "Big Joe Logsdon," removed from near the source of the north branch of the Potomac to Kentucky, and resided many years with the family of Andrew Barnett, in Greene County. He subsequently removed to Illinois.

Big Joe seems to have been a rare chap. Mr. Felix Renick has given some anecdotes of him in the *Western Pioneer*, in which he says:

> No Kentuckian could ever, with greater propriety than he, have said, "I can out-run, out-leap, out-jump, throw down, rag out, drag out and whip any man in the country."

The following is quoted from page 114, *School History of Kentucky*:

> Big Joe Logsdon's fight—A young man of giant frame and strength, and of reckless daring and adventure, removed to Kentucky and lived with Andy Barnett, in Green county. In 1790, the Indians attacked the settlement and drove all into the stockade fort near. Joe Logsdon's restless spirit longed for the woods, in spite of the dangerous foe. Venturing out on a hunt through the woods one day, heedless of warning, as he rode leisurely along a path, eating some grapes he had plucked, the ring of two rifles startled him and his horse. One bullet passed through the muscles of his breast, not disabling him much. The other ball killed his horse under him.
>
> He was on his feet in a moment, with rifle ready for action. He was a swift runner, and had boasted that he had often turned his back on an enemy. One huge Indian sprang on him after the shots, tomahawk in hand. Joe's reply drove him behind a tree. Just then he saw a smaller Indian behind another tree reloading his gun. A chance offered, and Joe fired and broke his protruding back. The big Indian now rushed forward to tomahawk him while his rifle was empty. The two giants met, and, alone in the forest, a desperate man-to-man battle for life and death took place. The struggle, long and exhausting, ended with Big Joe wrenching the knife of the savage from his hand, just as he had pulled it from his belt, and plunging it into the heart of the owner. Logsdon walked back to the fort pretty well satisfied to have come off so well. The dead Indians were found the next day.

Joe Logsdon would not allow anyone, white or Indian, to step in his way. He was a large and forceful man who could have his way in any circumstance. Most of those whom he confronted were intimidated by his sheer bulk, and no physical confrontation was ever needed or carried out.

Some years after Joe's altercation with the two Indians, peace with the Indians was restored. That frontier, like many others, became infested with a gang of outlaws, who commenced stealing horses and committing various depredations. To counteract which, a company of regulators, as they were called, was raised. In a contest between these and the depradators (plunderers), Big Joe Logsdon lost his life, which would not be highly esteemed in civil society. But in frontier settlements, which he always occupied, where savages and beasts were to be contended with for the right of soil, the use of such a man is very conspicuous. Without such, the country could never have been cleared of its natural rudeness, so as to admit the more brilliant and ornamental exercise of arts, sciences, and civilization.

The following statement proves that Joseph Logsdon's encounter was not just a "tall tale," but true.

> I, Roy A. Cann, the undersigned, wish to state that about twenty-five years ago I was at the home of Mr. Edward Pottenger who lived about one mile Northeast of Aetna Furnace, Hart County, at which time Mr. Pottenger told me the story of 'Big Joe' Logsdon's fight and the killing of two Indians, very much in the details as told in Collins' *History of Kentucky*. He said it was told to him by his mother, and that she showed him the graves of the Indians, which was pointed out to the writer by Mr. Pottenger.

Reverend William Jewel, Munfordville, Kentucky, says that his father told him about the same story, and that his father's land adjoined the Edward Pottenger farm. The location of the fight and the graves are on the lands of the Pottenger family, owned later by Joe, a son of Edward Pottenger. The first site of Mt. Zion Baptist Church is the location. Mt. Zion Church today is on its third location at Nigerdie, Hart County. The graves are about three hundred feet up the hill, just south of Lyn Camp Creek.

Joe and Susan raised a family of five children, Joe, Thomas, Prudence, Margaret and Susan. They evidently had many happy years together, until calamity struck. In 1832 there was a cholera epidemic that claimed three of their family members. Susan, a non-Catholic, died in the epidemic and is buried in Gold Hill Cemetery near Shawneetown, Illinois. Their son Joe, who also a died in the epidemic, is buried with his mother, and his tombstone is inscribed, "Joe

Logsdon Number Three." Young Joe had served in the Black Hawk War. Their daughter Margaret also perished in the epidemic. Obviously cholera is a debilitating disease. After an incubation period of 12 to 28 hours, the disease usually starts with an abrupt, painless, watery diarrhea that may amount to the volume of three to four gallons in 24 hours. Vomiting follows, and the patient rapidly becomes dehydrated. The patient may die of either dehydration or shock.

Here's what the Black Hawk War was all about. Black Hawk was a Sauk Indian in Illinois. The principal cause of the Indian troubles in 1831-32, better known as the Black Hawk War, was the determination of Black Hawk and his band to remain in their ancient villages, located on Rock River, not far from its junction with the Mississippi. The government having sometime previously, by various treaties, purchased the village and the whole country from the Sauk and Fox tribes of Indians, had some of these lands surveyed, and in 1828 some of the lands in and around the ancient village were sold; the collision of the two races for the possession of the property produced a disturbance between the Indians and the government. Seeing that war was inevitable, the Governor of Illinois made a call on the militia of the state for seven hundred men on May 26, 1831, and appointed Beardstown, on the Illinois River, as the place of rendezvous. The call was responded to with that promptness characteristic of the early pioneers of Illinois. Their habits of life were such that all were familiar with the rifle. After marching eight days, the mounted militia reached a point a few miles below the Sauk village on the Mississippi, where they joined the United States forces under General Gaines, and encamped in the evening. The next morning the forces marched up to the Indian town prepared to give the enemy battle; but in the night the Indians had escaped and crossed the Mississippi. This ended Black Hawk's bravado and his determination to die in his ancient village. The number of warriors under his command was estimated at from four to six hundred men. Black Hawk and his band landed on the west side of the Mississippi, a few miles below Rock Island, and camped there. General Gaines sent an order to him and his warriors that if he and his headmen did not come to Rock Island and make a treaty of peace, he would march his troops and give him battle at once. In a few days Black Hawk and the chiefs and headmen, 28 in number, appeared at Fort Armstrong, and on June 30, 1831, in full council with General Gaines and Governor John Reynolds, signed a treaty of peace.

During the winter of 1831-32 rumors were rife that Black Hawk and his band were dissatisfied, restless, and preparing for mischief. A chief of the Winnebago Indians who had a village on Rock river, some thirty miles above its confluence with the Mississippi, joined Black Hawk, who was located on the west bank of the Father of Waters. The chief had great influence with Black Hawk and his band. He made them believe that all the tribes on Rock river would join them, and that together they could bid defiance to the whites. By this unwise counsel Black Hawk resolved to re-cross the river, which he did in the winter of 1832. That move proved to be their destruction. Through his influence and zeal Black Hawk encouraged many of the Sauks and Foxes to join him at the head of his determined warriors. He first assembled them at old Fort Madison on the Mississippi; then subsequently he marched them up the river to the Yellow Banks, where he pitched his tent April 6, 1832. This armed array of savages soon alarmed the settlers, and a general panic spread through the whole frontier, from the Mississippi to Lake Michigan. Many settlers abandoned their homes and farms in terror, and the Governor decided, on April 16, to call out a large number of volunteers to operate in conjunction with General Atkinson, who was in command of the regular forces at Rock Island. The Governor ordered the troops to rendezvous at Beardstown on April 22.

To the stirring appeal of the Governor, the patriotic citizens of the state and Macon County nobly responded. Many of the best and most prominent men of the county enlisted to protect the frontier and preserve the honor of the state, and did perform service in the memorable events of the Black Hawk War.

The company consisted of mounted rangers, and became a part of the fifth regiment. Captain Johnson was promoted to the rank of Colonel, on May 16, and placed in command of the fifth regiment, and Lieutenant Pugh became a Captain. They were a part of the Brigade under command of General Samuel D. Whiteside. On May 12 they reached Dixon's ferry, where Jauor Stillman and his detachment of 275 men joined them; Stillman declined to join Whiteside's Brigade. Major Stillman and Baily received orders to go to "Old Man's Creek," now Stillman's Run, to ascertain the movements of the Indians. The two battalions camped about ten miles from the ferry on the evening of the 13th. The next morning Stillman took command of both battalions, continued the pursuit until sunset, when they camped in "front of a small creek," (Stillman's Run), about thirty miles from Dixon. Black Hawk, learning of their approach, sent out three men to escort them to his camp, that a council might be held; but the men were taken prisoners. Five others were sent out for the same purpose, but two of them were killed. This aroused Black Hawk, and with about forty men he met the assailants—the main body of his warriors being about ten miles away—and routed them completely, and in great confusion.

Captain William Warnick organized the second Company in the summer of 1832. It was called "The Rangers." The company was fifty strong. They enlisted for sixty days, and furnished their own horses, arms, ammunition, and provisions. This company was organized for the protection of the frontier counties. They left Decatur June 4, 1832, and marched to where Monticello, Illinois, now stands, where they went into camp. While here they learned that the Indian village of Kickapoo near the head of the Big Vermillion, had been deserted by the warriors, who had gone to assist Black Hawk, and they left their squaws, pappooses, and a few old men in charge of the village. The company proceeded to the village, but found that it had been entirely deserted about three days before their arrival. At the expiration of the sixty days, Captain Warnick and men returned to their homes, but were told to hold themselves in readiness for further service. They were finally discharged 113 days after their enlistment. Each man of this company received for his services, $52.00, and a land warrant for 160 acres of land.

The force marched to the mouth of Rock River, where General Atkinson received the volunteers into the United States service and assumed command. Black Hawk and his warriors were still up on the Rock River.

The army under Atkinson commenced its march up the river on May 9. Governor Reynolds, the gallant "Old Ranger," remained with the army, and the President recognized him as a Major General, and he was paid accordingly. His presence in the army did much toward harmonizing and conciliating those jealousies that generally exist between volunteers and regular troops. Major John A. Wakefield and Colonel Ewing acted as spies for a time in the campaign of 1832, to discover the location of the enemy, if possible. A Mr. Kinney acted as guide for them; he understood the Sauk dialect. On May 14, 1832 Major Stillman's command had a sort of running battle with the Indians at or near what is now known as Stillman's Run, a small, sluggish stream. In this engagement eleven white men and eight Indians were killed. Black Hawk and warriors fought with the spirit born of desperation. Black Hawk says in his book that he tried at Stillman's Run to call back his warriors, as he thought the whites were making a sham retreat in order to draw him into an ambush of the whole army under General Whiteside. The hasty retreat and rout of Stillman and his army was, in a measure, demoralizing to the entire forces. Undoubtedly the cause of the defeat was a lack of discipline. When Governor Reynolds learned of the disaster of Major Stillman, he at once ordered out two thousand additional volunteers. With that promptitude characteristic of the old "War Govenor," he wrote out by candle-light on the evening of Stillman's defeat, the order for the additional troops, and by daylight dispatched John Ewing, Robert Blackwell, and John A. Wakefiield to distribute the order to the various counties. The volunteers again promptly responded; however, the soldiers from Macon County did but little fighting. On July 10 the army disbanded for want of provisions. General Scott arrived soon after with a large force at the post of Chicago, to effect, if possible, a treaty with the Indians. Small detachments of Black Hawk's warriors would persistently hang on the outskirts of the main body of the army, thieve and plunder, and pounce upon and kill the lonely sentinel or straggling soldier. On July 15 the soldiers were reviewed, and those incapable of duty were discharged and returned home. Poquette, a half-breed, and a Winnebago called the "White Pawnee" were selected for guides to the camp of Black Hawk and his band. Several battles and skirmishes occurred with the enemy, the principal of which was on the banks of the Mississippi, where the warriors fought with great desperation. Over one hundred and fifty were killed in the engagement, and large numbers drowned in attempting to swim the river. After the battle the volunteers were marched to Dixon, where they were discharged. This ended the campaign and the Black Hawk War. At the battle of the Bad Axe, Black Hawk and some of his warriors escaped the Americans, and had gone up on the Wisconsin River, but he subsequently surrendered himself. Fort Armstrong, on Rock Island, was the place appointed where a treaty would be made with the Indians, but before it was effected, that dreadful scourge, the cholera of 1832, visited not only the regular army, depleting its ranks far more rapidly than the balls of the Indians had done, but it also sought out its many victims in the dusky bands of the Black Hawk tribe.

On September 15, 1832 a treaty was made with the Winnebago Indians. They sold out all their lands in Illinois and all south of the Wisconsin river and west of Green Bay, and the government gave them a large district of country west of the Mississippi, and ten thousand dollars a year for seven years, oxen, agricultural implements, etc.

On September 21, 1832, a treaty was made with all the Sauk and Fox tribes, on which they ceded to the United States the tract of country on which a few years afterwards the State of Iowa was formed. In consideration of the above cession of lands, the government gave them an annuity of twenty thousand dollars for thirty years, forty kegs of tobacco and forty barrels of salt, more gunsmiths, blacksmith shop, etc., and six thousand bushels of corn for immediate support, mostly intended for the Black Hawk band.

The treaties above mentioned terminated favorably, and the security resulting therefrom gave a new and rapid impetus to the development of the state, and now enterprising towns and villages, and beautiful farms, adorn the rich and alluvial prairies that before were only desecrated by the wild bands who inhabited them. Agricultural pursuits, commerce and manufactures, churches and schools, are lending their influence to advance an intelligent and prosperous people. (The foregoing details of the Black Hawk War were taken from pages 80-81 of the *History of Macon County, Illinois*.) Although the Logsdons were a hearty bunch, having survived the Black Hawk War, they weren't hearty enough to avoid the cholera epidemic.

So, how did he get the other nickname, "Bulger Joe"? Mrs. Hazel A. Spraker, a descendant of Ruth Logsdon, wrote that her uncle, Judge J. H. Atterbury of Litchfield, Illinois, wrote her in 1931:

> Zack and Charlie Kessinger were in attendance at a Kessinger Reunion. Zack is 84 years old and Charles a few years younger and both have splendid memories of the days gone by. They tell me that Bulger Joe Logsdon and his history are familiar to both of them. Both say that Joe Logsdon went from Kentucky to Illinois. He was in the neighborhood of Peoria, Illinois where he met Indian forces superior to his own and the latter was forced to retreat. Joe was defending the rear of his forces and when the van (vanguard) came to the Wabash River between Illinois and Indiana, they found the river to be flooded. They were waiting for Joe to solve their predicament. On Joe's arrival, he readily saw the danger, with the hostile forces pressing from the rear and the swollen river ahead. He promptly gave orders to 'bulger' the stream (presumably meaning to swim the river). His men promptly did so, but the redskins were afraid to try and the whites were thereby saved. He was thereafter called Bulger Joe.

Joseph Logsdon does not show up in the 1810 census, probably because the following is found in the Circuit Court of Green County, Kentucky: On November 24, 1794, Court was called and held for the examination of Joseph Logsdon for a felony.

> The said Joseph Logsdon who stands committed to jail accused of stealing a horse, the property of William Vaunce, was brought into Court, and pleaded NOT guilty. Sundry witnesses were sworn and examined and the prisoner heard in defense. It is the opinion of the Court he is not guilty of said offense and he is discharged."

About four months later, he was again brought to trial and this time he was supposed to have stolen the horse from Andrew Barnett. Then a third entry in the Court records says he stole the horse from a Mr. Owens. The cases were all dismissed and Joseph went to Illinois.

"Big Joe," or "Bulger Joe," exemplified the early pioneer and went well beyond the ordinary adventuresome trailblazer. If his life does not clearly show the hardiness of Father Durbin's ancestors, it is doubtful that anything will.

Kentucky pioneers cleared the way for Father Durbin to proceed with his geographically generous ministry. Daniel Boone was also instrumental in subduing the Indian menace in Kentucky, paving the way for Father Durbin to minister in relative safety.

Chapter 3

▼

A Boone to Society

Big Joe Logsdon was a true pioneer, and certainly Daniel Boone was too. About fifty years before the Reverend Father Elisha John Durbin began practicing his Kentucky ministry, there was a powerful frontiersman who was making Kentucky safe for that ministry. That frontiersman was Daniel Boone. It seems fitting to tell the story of the famous pioneer because his efforts really did pave the way for Father Durbin to roam through most of what is now Kentucky without the fear of marauding Indians to make his life difficult. Let us begin.

The Daniel Boone Homestead was settled in 1730 by the frontiersman's parents. Daniel Boone was born here November 2, 1734 and lived his first 16 years in Berks County, Pennsylvania. It was a log farmhouse that evolved into, and was replaced by, the main house of the Daniel Boone Homestead, situated east of Reading in Berks County. When Boone lived here, English Quaker, German, Swiss, Huguenot and Swedish pioneers sparsely populated the area. (The Huguenots were French Protestants.) The mid-18th century structure that survives today is built over the spring and cellar

Daniel Boone Homestead

where the first Boone log cabin stood and where young Daniel Boone lived before his family moved to North Carolina. Today, the historic site tells the story not only of the early life of Daniel Boone, but also the saga of the region's settlers by comparing and contrasting the lifestyles of different cultures in 18th century rural Pennsylvania.

The name Daniel Boone will forever be synonymous with the saga of the American frontier. Boone was the inveterate wayfarer who achieved lasting fame guiding land-hungry settlers to the Kentucky frontier and fighting to defend them against Indian attack. More than any other man, Daniel Boone was responsible for the exploration and settlement of Kentucky. His grandfather came from England to America in 1717. His father, also from England, was a weaver and blacksmith, and he raised livestock in the country near Reading, Pennsylvania.

If Daniel Boone was destined to become a man of the wild, an explorer of unmapped spaces, his boyhood was the perfect preparation. He came to know the friendly Indians in the forests, and early he was marking the habits of wild things and bringing them down with a crude whittled spear. When he was twelve his father gave him a rifle, and his career as a huntsman began.

Kentucky was once a district that geographically formed the vastly superior portion of Fincastle County, Virginia. From here Dr. Thomas Walker, in 1758, and John Findlay, in 1767, set out to explore this district, and in so doing, Dr. Walker discovered the Cumberland Mountain range and the river of the same name. Findlay's excursion was for the sole purpose of establishing some sort of trade with the Indians, but he found them too hostile and returned home. Some of these facts are contained in Webb's *The Centenary of Catholicity in Kentucky*. It was Findlay's adventure that inspired Daniel Boone to explore the country that lay beyond the Cumberland Mountains.

Daniel Boone was a noble adventurer and perhaps the most famous of the Kentucky pioneers. (His ancestors were among the original Catholic settlers of Maryland and he undoubtedly inherited his stern virtues from them.) It was through his fortitude and bravery that Kentucky became safe enough for the early settlers to establish their homes there. Father Durbin's ministry would be relatively safe from those early bands of dangerous Indians that so plagued his forebears, including the likes of his grandfather, Christopher Durbin, "Big Joe" Logsdon, and even Daniel Boone himself.

As we mentioned, Daniel Boone was born in 1734, and Christopher Durbin in 1741, seven years apart. From North Carolina, through the Cumberland Gap, Boone first came to the land now known as Kentucky in 1767 on a hunting expedition, returning there to hunt again in 1769. (As described in *The New Encyclopaedia Britannica Micropaedia*, the Cumberland Gap is a notch in the Appalachian Mountains near the juncture of Virginia, Tennessee and Kentucky.) Daniel fell in love with this relatively unexplored land, and in 1773 he returned once again, bringing settlers, including his own family, with him. This time he would remain in Kentucky.

Chester Harding, *Daniel Boone*, 1820

Christopher Durbin brought his family to Kentucky in 1779, six years after Daniel's latest arrival there, by way of North Carolina and the Wilderness Road. In 1775, while employed by Richard Henderson's Transylvania Company, Daniel Boone and 28 companions built the Wilderness Road which ran from eastern Virginia deep into the interior of Kentucky to Boonesboro (*The New Encyclopaedia Britannica Micropaedia*). It is entirely likely that Daniel and Christopher were well-acquainted with one another, and both of them were considered to be early Kentucky pioneers.

Daniel's father, Squire Boone, was an English Quaker born in Devonshire in 1696. While still a youth, Squire, his brother George and sister Sarah embarked for Philadelphia to appraise the possibilities of a settlement for their father's family, who finally immigrated in 1717.

Squire settled first in Abington, and then moved to Gwynedd, where he met Sarah Morgan, born in 1700 to Welsh Quakers. Married July 23, 1720, they lived first near Gwynedd, then in Chalfont, Bucks County, before purchasing 250 acres for the Homestead in 1730. Squire's father and brothers also lived in the area and became prominent in business, local government and the Friends Meeting (also called Quakers).

The children of Squire and Sarah were Sarah, Israel, Samuel, Jonathan, Elizabeth, Mary, Daniel, George, Edward, Squire and Hannah, all born at Otey,

Pennsylvania. Daniel was the sixth child and was born November 2, 1734. Edward was killed by Indians when 36 years old, and Squire died at the age of 76. The four daughters married. (Squire's father was George Boone III, and his mother was Mary Milton Maugridge. They all came to America from England.)

Although little is known of Daniel's Pennsylvania years, he undoubtedly helped his father as farmer, weaver and blacksmith and had the usual experiences of a boy growing up in the backcountry.

In 1750 Squire and Sarah joined the growing southward movement of Pennsylvanians, and concluded their long trek in the Yadkin Valley of North Carolina. While their principal motive may have been economic, it is also a fact that Squire had been "read out of Meeting" by the Exeter Friends in 1748 for his being unrepentant in allowing his son Israel to marry a non-Quaker.

Daniel was then only 15½ years old when the family moved to the Yadkin Valley, but ahead was a life filled with the rigors of the American frontier. At nineteen or twenty he left his family home with a military expedition in the French and Indian War. In the spring of 1756 he married Rebecca Bryan, daughter of Joseph Bryan, and with her, when he was home, raised ten children. In 1773 he failed in his first attempt to settle Kentucky, but in 1775 he succeeded in establishing Boonesboro. Between 1775 and 1783 Daniel Boone was a leader among settlers in opening new parts of Kentucky and in resisting Indian raids. Christopher Durbin surely must have appreciated Boone's leadership, as Christopher and his family arrived in Kentucky during this same period. Although Boone lost two sons and a brother in the fighting, he was merciful and compassionate toward his native adversaries.

North Carolina was the home of Daniel's boyhood, his young manhood and the State in which he chose his wife. He and his family lived in a valley bordering on the South Yadkin River there. He was known as a "Road-Builder, town-maker and Commonwealth founder," and when Kentucky had representation in Virginia, Boone sat in the House of Commons as a Burgess.

Following is a list of the children of Daniel and Rebecca.

James Boone was born in 1757. In 1773 he was tortured and murdered by Indians while crossing Clinch Mountain in Virginia during the family's first attempt to reach Kentucky. Following this tragedy, the survivors turned back.

Israel Boone was born in 1759 and died in the Battle of Blue Licks, Kentucky in 1782.

Susannah Boone was born in 1760 and died in 1800 in St. Charles County, Missouri, the year in which Father Elisha John Durbin was born. She married William Hays who was born in 1754 and died in 1804.

Jemima Boone, born in 1762, married Flanders Callaway who was born in 1758 in Virginia and died in 1824. He was the son of James Callaway.

Levina Boone, born in 1766 and died in 1802 in Clark County, Kentucky, married Joseph Scholl who was born in 1755 and died in 1835.

Rebecca Boone was born in 1768 and died in 1805 in Clark County, Kentucky. She married Philip Goe who was born in 1767 and died in Kentucky in 1805.

Daniel Morgan Boone was born in 1769 and died in 1839 in Jackson County, Missouri. He married Sarah Griffin Lewis. She was born in 1786 and died in 1850.

Jesse Bryan Boone, born in 1773 and died in 1820 in St. Louis Missouri, married Chloe Van Bibber. She was born in 1772.

William Boone, born in 1775, died in infancy.

Nathan Boone was born in 1781 and died in 1856 in Kentucky. He married Olive Van Bibber who was born in 1783 in Kentucky and died in 1858 in Missouri. According to the *The New Encyclopaedia Britannica Micropaedia*, the city of Montana in Boone County, central Iowa, was renamed Boone, Iowa in 1871 in honor of Daniel's son, Captain Nathan Boone.

In a history brief that aired on television's History Channel in late December 1998, it was said that Daniel's younger brother, Squire Boone, invented the first fire extinguisher. He was somehow able to insert a water-filled canister into the barrel of his rifle, and when the rifle was fired at flames, the canister would burst, extinguishing the fire. A Baptist church was established in Bardstown, Kentucky, in 1781, and Squire Boone, Daniel's brother, reportedly traveled to Louisville to preach the city's first Baptist Sermon.

Daniel Boone did not fight in the Revolutionary war. Instead, he was busy fighting Indians in Kentucky. Daniel Boone did as much or more service for our country in fighting Indians and keeping them back as if he had served in the war with General George Washington. Like Washington, Boone was a surveyor. He surveyed nearly all the land in Kentucky. He was also a law maker, having passed a law for the protection of game in Kentucky and also one for keeping up the breed of fine horses.

In 1767 Boone traveled into the edge of Kentucky and camped for the winter at Salt Spring near Prestonsburg. But the least explored parts were still farther west, beyond the Cumberlands, and John Finley persuaded Daniel to go on a great adventure.

On May 1, 1769, accompanied by John Findlay and four others, Boone reached the Red River in eastern Kentucky where they erected a cabin. They had passed Cumberland Gap and on the 7th of June, they set up camp at Station Camp creek. Colonel Daniel Boone spent the winter of 1769-1770 in a cave, on the waters of Shawnee, in Mercer county. A tree marked with his name, is yet standing near the head of the cave. After a few months, Indians captured Boone and another member of the party, John Stuart, but after a few days they escaped and returned to camp only to discover that it had been destroyed. A few days later, Daniel's younger brother, Squire Boone, joined them. Soon after this addition to the party, Stuart was shot and scalped by Indians. This event seemed to strengthen the bond between the brothers, Daniel and Squire, who continued roving the area that is now Kentucky. For three years, until March 1771, Daniel Boone remained away from his family, never beholding the face of a white man, except for his brother and the friends who had been killed (*The Centenary of Catholicity in Kentucky*). During his time away from home he explored Kentucky as far west as the Falls of the Ohio, where Louisville is now. There was another visit to Kentucky in 1773, and in 1774 he built a cabin at Harrodsburg. On this trip, Boone followed the Kentucky River to its mouth.

In the fall of 1773, Boone headed another expedition that consisted of forty men. As they neared the Cumberland Mountains they were attacked by Indians and a bloody battle ensued. The Indians were driven off, but six members of Boone's party were killed or wounded.

In 1775, while building the Wilderness Road near its termination at Boonesboro, Boone and his party were attacked by Indians and a number of his companions were killed.

Boonesboro today is a resort village in Clark county, Kentucky, on the Kentucky River, nine miles southwest of Winchester. It is the site of Fort Boonesboro, built in 1775 by Daniel Boone and a company of North Carolina men under Colonel Richard Henderson who had just opened Boone's Trace (an offshoot of the Wilderness Road) through the Cumberland (Mountains) Gap. The group, under a grant from the Cherokees (regarded as illegal by Britain and Virginia), claimed all the land between the Kentucky and Cumberland rivers which they called Transylvania. The Transylvania Convention held at the fort in May 1775 was the first legislative assembly west of the Appalachians. During the Revolutionary War the settlement was under constant Indian attack. Here the first marriage in Kentucky took place on Aug. 7, 1776, between Samuel Henderson, younger brother of the pioneer, and Betsy Calloway (who, along with her sister, Fanny, and Boone's daughter, Jemima, had just been rescued from the Indians). The fort, which was abandoned in 1778 after withstanding a Shawnee Indian attack, has been reconstructed within Fort Boonesboro State Park and includes blockhouses, craft shops, and a museum. The population in 1990 was 1,885.

In 1775, having been engaged as the agent of a Carolina trading company to establish a road by which colonists could reach Kentucky and settle there, Boone built a stockade and fort on the site of Boonesboro. The first group of settlers crossed the Cumberland Gap to Boonesboro by the road established by Boone, later called the "Wilderness Road". During the American Revolution the community suffered repeated attacks, and in 1778 Indian raiders took Boone captive temporarily. The settlement, however, was eventually established as a permanent village. Colonel Richard Henderson of the Transylvania Company had hired Boone as his agent, and March, 1775 is when Boone came again to the "Great Meadow" with a party of thirty settlers.

Sketch of Daniel Boone

As for the continued skirmishes with Indians, Betsy and Fanny, two of the daughters of Colonel Richard Calloway, a Kentucky pioneer, were captured with Jemima, Boone's second daughter, in a boat at Boonesboro, Kentucky, on July 17, 1776. The girls' screams alerted the men in the fort, and Boone quickly formed a party of only eight men and gave chase. The girls were recovered unharmed on the third day after their capture when Boone and his party surprised the captors (*The Centenary of Catholicity in Kentucky*).

Indians killed Daniel's two eldest sons, James and Israel, and the three younger sons, Jesse Bryan, William and Nathan, later migrated to Missouri.

It seems that Daniel Boone spent a good deal of his time evading tribes of Indians as he explored the Kentucky wilderness back in the 1700s. While pausing to rest one day in an old log cabin used for curing tobacco, Daniel spied several Indians approaching. Quickly he climbed up into the overhead loft with the drying tobacco leaves. In doing so he lost his coonskin cap and it fell to the cabin floor. There was no time to retrieve it so Boone lay quietly as the Indians entered the building and sat down to rest. But they quickly jumped to their feet when the keen eyes of one Indian spied the cap. The Kentucky scout knew he would soon be discovered so he crashed down through the tobacco, thrashing his arms about. Bits of dried tobacco filled the air and got into the eyes of the startled Indians. While they were rubbing their smarting eyes and howling with pain, Daniel ran from the cabin and safely disappeared into the nearby woods.

By 1783, thanks to Daniel Boone and the other pioneers of that day, the people venturing into Kentucky no longer had to fear molestation by the Indians.

The publication of Daniel Boone's *Adventures* in 1784 served to immortalize Boone the frontiersman as an American legend and a true folk hero. Published by John Filson on Boone's 50th birthday, the narrative describes in Boone's own words his exploits in the Kentucky wilderness from May, 1769 to October of 1782. *The Adventures of Colonel Daniel Boone* was subsequently published in *The American Magazine* in 1787 and again in a book by George Imlay in 1793. In his autobiographical narrative Boone tells of his passage through the Cumberland Gap, leading a party of settlers that cut the Wilderness Road in 1775.

Boone's trailblazing efforts opened a door beyond the Allegheny Mountains, establishing a route used by thousands in the first westward migration. In his *Adventures* Boone—a colonel in the Virginia militia—describes his founding of Boonesboro on the Kentucky River, his capture by the Shawnee Indians, his adoption by Chief Black Fish as his son, and his daring escape on foot through the forests covering 160 miles in four days. In putting pen to paper, America's most famous of all "long hunters" recounts events of singular courage during this eventful 13-year period of his life, providing us with a fascinating account.

Here's how those early settlers lived. As time passed on, families that were previously cooped up in a particular fort or station would emerge from its gates and set up a life for themselves beyond its protecting palisades. Not a few of these paid with their lives for their temerity; but there were many who were left undisturbed to pursue their peaceful avocations, and to win for themselves comfortable homes in the wilderness. Having made a survey, the first thing they did was to clear a favorable spot of its forest growth and to erect in its center a rude structure of logs. The size of the cabin was made to correspond with the number of persons who were to find shelter under its roof. Generally speaking, it was divided into two rooms, but often into three or four. The roof was formed of clapboards, and the floor, where there was other than the naked earth, of rough-hewn lumber. The openings for the introduction of light were lateral slits in the wall, generally three feet in length by one foot in width, and though they were sometimes protected from the inside by hanging wooden shutters, they had no sash or glass.

The furniture used in these primitive times was all improvised on the call of necessity. It ordinarily consisted of a table fashioned after the pattern of a butcher's block; bedsteads constructed of upright and lateral sections of young timber, dovetailed at the corners; wooden benches and three-legged stools. In a corner of one of the rooms, under a shed of boughs in the rear of the cabin, were to be found a hominy-mortar and a hand-mill for grinding corn. Wooden platters served the purposes to which earthenware is now devoted, and the easily cultivated gourd made an admirable drinking cup (*The Centenary of Catholicity in Kentucky*).

It is not to be doubted that the emigrants had from the start pretty clear notions of the privations they would have to endure, and of the hardships their ventures would entail upon them. But never were men and women less dainty or more courageous. They met discomforts without complaint, and they shrank from no character of toil that gave promise of beneficial results to themselves or to others. One of their most serious troubles referred to the long and often dangerous journeys they were obliged to make to the salt licks in order to procure supplies of salt. There were no roads, blazed trees being the only guides to direct the messengers to and from the licks.

For protection against cold, whether in sleeping or journeying, the emigrants had recourse to the skins of beasts, killed in the chase or trapped on the margins of the watercourses. The art of dressing and rendering these pliable was of common knowledge at the time. A serious inconvenience of the settlers arose from the fact that there were no mills in the country for the grinding of corn. The reduction of grain into meal by the use of the old-fashioned hand-mill was a laborious process, and it involved so much of the time and labor of the households, that measures were almost immediately taken, after the country was supposed to be free from Indians, to remedy the annoyance. Rude corn mills, very simple affairs, were put up in the vicinity of some of the stations as early as the year 1780. It was not until about the year 1790, however, that a more pretentious mode of milling was established in the State. About the year named, a little earlier or a little later, mills were put up in Bardstown, on Cartwright's creek, and on the Rolling Fork, to which the Catholic settlers of Nelson and Washington Counties were in the habit of repairing with their grist for grinding.

It will not be amiss to note how little there was of complexity in the styles of dress worn by both men and women in the olden times in Kentucky. "As late as 1782," says a writer on the subject, "the men dressed in pioneer homespun; moccasins and leather leggings for the lower extremities; hats made of splinters rolled in buffalo wool and sewed with deer sinews or buckskin whangs (rawhides); shirts and hunting shirts of buckskin. A few dressed in Indian costume—wore nothing whatever but breechclouts. The females wore a coarse cloth made of buffalo wool; underwear of dressed deerskin; sun-bonnets something like the men's hats; moccasins in winter; but in summer all went barefooted."

From and after the year 1785, the underwear of both sexes was invariably of flax linen, and a young woman could be said to be in full dress when she appeared in a closely-fitting gown of cotton, woven in stripes, or of half-bleached flax linen, five yards to the pattern, for summer; or in one of linsey-woolsey, dyed to suit her individual taste with coloring matter gathered by herself from the neighboring woods. From top to toe—from her sun-bonnet, stiffened with hickory splints, to her moccasined feet—she was able to boast that her wearing apparel was the creation of her own busy fingers.

Life in early Kentucky settlements

Daniel Boone soon became a legend. He had established Fort Boonesboro, which later became the city of Boonesboro (spelled "Boonesborough" in those early days). Today, Boonesboro is located just a few miles southeast of the large city of Lexington, Kentucky. The very first settlements in Kentucky were Harrod's Town, Benjamin Logan's, and Boonesboro. When Boone brought his wife and daughter to Boonesboro, they were considered to be the first white women in Kentucky. In Missouri, the city and county seat of Cooper County was settled in 1810 and renamed Boonville in honor of Daniel Boone (*The New Encyclopaedia Britannica Micropaedia*).

Boone left the Bluegrass in 1788 and moved into what is now West Virginia. Ten years later he again heard the call of unknown country luring him, this time to the Missouri region. As his dugout canoe passed Cincinnati, somebody asked why he was leaving Kentucky. "Too crowded" was his answer. Twice, Boone returned to visit his boyhood home—in 1781 and in 1788—a hero and legend in his day. Though his legend grew, his finances languished. Beset by creditors and personal disillusion, Boone finally left Kentucky in 1799 for Missouri, where he died at St. Charles, near St. Louis, on September 26, 1820 at the age of 85.

He was buried beside his wife in Missouri. A quarter of a century later they were brought back to the Bluegrass and laid to rest in Frankfort's cemetery. There they rest, on a bluff above the river and town, on a "high, far-seeing place" like the ones he always climbed to see the land beyond—a monument to the new country in the wilderness that they had helped to explore and settle.

It was the likes of these men—pioneers—that included Daniel Boone and Christopher Durbin who broke down the barriers to civilization in Kentucky. He certainly didn't know it at the time, but Christopher Durbin would have a grandson, Elisha Durbin, who would be able to carry on his pastoral duties without the fear of being killed by Indians. Although safe from Indians, we shall now see how Kentucky took its toll on Father Durbin in other ways. Now that the foundation for civilization in Kentucky is set, the story of the life of Father Elisha John Durbin resumes.

CHAPTER 4

THE PRIMORDIAL

Side by side with the legendary Daniel Boones and Davy Crocketts who opened up the vast tangled wilderness of the Western frontier to settlement in the early 1800s were historic priest-missionaries of at least equal stature. When the forests of Kentucky became the new frontier soon after the close of the Revolutionary War, many Catholics from Maryland established congregations that a breed of wilderness missionaries grew up in whose like has seldom been seen before or since. One of these frontier priests, and among the most amazing missionaries in the history of the United States, was the Reverend Elisha John Durbin.

References for this chapter include *The Catholic Advocate* (Louisville, 1836-1887); *The Record* (Louisville, 1879-1887); Hawlett, *Historical Tribute to St. Thomas Seminary* (St. Louis, 1906); *Catholic Builders of Our Land* (Reverend John B. Ebel); and *Heroes of Christ* (author not given).

Father Elisha John Durbin was born about 16 miles above Boonesboro, Kentucky. Boonesboro, named for the frontiersman Daniel Boone, was still in the heart of the Kentucky wilderness. Boonesboro is about 15 miles southeast of Lexington, which was also a young settlement at that time. When a boy, he went to church with his parents at Saint Francis Church in Scott County, Kentucky. The pastor then was Reverend Robert Angier OSD, who spoke in terms of endearment of young Elisha (*The Centenary of Catholicity in Kentucky*). In later years, Father Durbin would speak of Reverend Angier with unstinted praise.

John Baptist David, born in 1761 in a little town on the River Loire, in France, between the cities of Nantes and Angers, founded the Seminary of St. Thomas. He attended the diocesan seminary in Nantes and was ordained a deacon in 1783 when he went to Paris, where, for the next two years he continued his theological studies. He was raised to the priesthood on September 24, 1785. His superiors then sent him to the diocesan seminary at Angers where he taught philosophy, theology and the scriptures for the next four years. The storm of the French Revolution settled over Angers, and in late 1790 the seminary was seized by the revolutionary troops and converted into an arsenal. Students and teachers alike were forced to flee. For two years Reverend David stayed in a private French home when he decided to sail for America. He wanted to help with the infant and struggling missions there, so he taught himself English as best he could. On this voyage Bishop Benedict Joseph Flaget and Father Theodore Badin accompanied him. Reverend David served in Maryland under Bishop Carroll for a while, and when his dear friend, soon-to-be Bishop Flaget was assigned to Bardstown, Kentucky, Reverend David accompanied him as an assistant. The Bardstown diocese needed a seminary, and Bishop Flaget charged Father David, a rigid disciplinarian, with this assignment. With a little help, Father David erected a small (18 by 24 feet) log cabin that was to become the seminary. Father David would later become Bishop of Bardstown, the first American bishop to be consecrated west of Baltimore. (*The Centenary of Catholicity in Kentucky*.)

The Bardstown area, originally called Salem, was explored in the mid 1770s. In 1780, William Bard paid a visit to the area acting as agent for his brother David and John C. Owings. In 1785, he "laid off" Bardstown from an original land grant of 1000 acres issued by the Virginia General Assembly. That same year, the first courthouse was built, made out of hewn logs. The town, originally called Baird's Town (a variation of the family name), was designated Bardstown when incorporated in 1788.

Bardstown is the county seat of Nelson County, named in honor of one-time governor of Virginia, Thomas Nelson. Nelson was the fourth county erected in the district (now state) of Kentucky.

Also known as the "Bourbon Capital of the World" the area in and around Bardstown once reflected 22 operating distilleries with distilling records dating back to 1776. The city was also the trade center for a fertile agricultural area, growing tobacco, grain, livestock and dairy products. Coincidentally, Basil Hayden, who figures prominently in the Durbin family ancestry, came to this area from Maryland in 1785, accompanied by twenty-five families along with a Catholic priest. Among this group were the Cissell, Tucker, Moore, Knott and Mattingly families and William and Basil Hayden. They held the first Catholic mass west of the Appalachian Mountains. Some went on to Missouri about 1803 before the Louisiana Purchase in 1804 from the French. Basil Hayden began distilling a very smooth bourbon in 1796 in Kentucky. Basil Hayden Bourbon can be found today in some liquor stores, but in today's economy, Basil Hayden Bourbon is quite expensive, currently selling for between $40 and $50 for a 750ml bottle.

One can also get the feel for the importance that religion and education have played in Bardstown's history by visiting Spalding Hall, a building of the old St. Joseph College and the adjacent St. Joseph Proto-Cathedral, the first Catholic Cathedral west of the Allegheny Mountains. The Trappists' Abbey of Our Lady of Gethsemane, founded in 1848 is also in the city.

In 1785, groups of Maryland Catholics began an inner trek, away from the coast, and toward the West. Within 25 years their numbers on the frontier had grown so steadily that in 1810 a bishop—Benedict Joseph Flaget—had been consecrated for this people. The oldest inland American Catholic diocese was underway.

So much was distinctive about these Kentucky Catholics. Their first parish, Holy Cross, was gathered together by lay leadership who urgently sought a priest from Bishop Carroll in Baltimore. Their first seminary, St. Thomas, began literally on a flatboat floating down the Ohio River; on board regular lessons and religious exercises were held. One of their first colleges—St. Mary's—was founded in an old whiskey distillery building.

When the new American Republic began, and during most of the "Federal Period" of American history, Catholics with their single diocesan headquarters at Baltimore, had constituted less than one percent of the populace. Then came the four new dioceses of Boston, New York, Philadelphia and Bardstown, and a process of growth was in operation that would see the old faith constituted as the largest religious grouping in the nation by the end of the nineteenth century.

Kentucky—the fifteenth colony—was the first western star in the American flag when it entered the Union in 1792. Soon the new commonwealth was boasting many national western "firsts," including the premier Catholic cathedral, colleges, academies, seminary, religious sisterhoods and contemplative abbey. All was centered around the thriving little urban hub of Bardstown, nerve center of a growing benevolent empire of faith, worship and service.

Bardstown is Kentucky's second oldest city and today plays host to many historic and popular attractions, including My Old Kentucky Home State Park. Following a visit to the mansion known as Federal Hill, home of three Kentucky governors, the great composer Stephen Foster wrote the popular ballad, *My Old Kentucky Home* in 1853. It became Kentucky's state song.

During the Civil War, in September 1862, General Braxton Bragg's Confederate forces occupied Bardstown. There will be more about Father Durbin's involvement in the Civil War later in this book.

The new diocese was vast, considerably larger than the country of France. It spread from the Great Lakes to the Deep South; from the Mississippi to the Alleghenies. Over thirty other dioceses would eventually be taken from the Bardstown territory as from a solicitous mother: such later urban centers of faith as Chicago, Detroit, Nashville, Indianapolis, Cincinnati and Memphis.

If the earliest lay leaders were to trace their roots to proud old British stock, the first long-term clerical leaders of Catholic Kentucky were of French extraction. Many were, in fact, exiles from the French Revolution, those who refused to take the oath that would make of the church a mere arm of an all-encompassing state.

In 1816 young Elisha Durbin entered the preparatory seminary of St. Thomas in Nelson County, Kentucky, where he studied under such distinguished missionaries as Bishop Flaget, Father Felix de Andreis CM; and Father Joseph Rosati CM who later became Bishop of St. Louis, Missouri. As was customary in those days of frontier life, Elisha spent about half of his time in manual labor at the institution, contributing to its support. That was the rule of the seminary (*The Centenary of Catholicity in Kentucky*). A background sketch of Bishop Flaget seems in order here.

Late in 1841 the saintly old Bishop Flaget began the move of the center of administration from the town of Bardstown to the much larger and growing riverport of Louisville. It was at that time that the old prelate made one of the first uses of an image that lingers still: that of the Bardstown area as a Holy Land. From Bardstown as from a little Bethlehem, the church must move forth and enter into a new era.

So in one sense the Bardstown era ended as a phase in American Catholic history. Immigrant, urban and national realities were pressing in. And yet, in a truer sense, the Bardstown era can never end in Kentucky Catholicism. Geographically, emotionally, spiritually, the Kentucky Holy Land remains today a place of rare beauty, personalities and spiritual presence (*Catholic Encyclopedia*, Volume 5, viewed at the Newberry Library, Chicago, Illinois). In fact, a map of modern Bardstown and its environs shows communities named Holy Cross, Nazareth, St. Catherine, Nerinx, Loretto, St. Francis, St. Mary and St. Thomas. (St. Thomas, presumably the site of the original seminary where Father Durbin studied for the priesthood, is just south of modern Bardstown's city limits.)

America is often said to be a place devoid of many places of strong romantic and emotional appeal. For American Catholicism, at least, Bardstown and its Holy Land must remain a highly notable exception.

Most of the foregoing historical sketch is from *The Faithful Image* by Clyde F. Crews

Benedict Joseph Flaget was born November 7, 1763 in Contournat, France and died February 11, 1850 in Louisville, Kentucky. He was most certainly an influential figure in the development of the Roman Catholic Church in the United States. Bishop Flaget entered the Sulpician Society, was ordained in 1786 or 1787, and taught theology. He was one of several Sulpicians sent in 1792 to establish the first Roman Catholic seminary in the United States. During the next 17 years he served as missionary to Vincennes, Indiana.

Bishop John Carroll's diocese of the United States was divided in 1808, and he consecrated Flaget on November 4, 1810 as the first bishop of Bardstown, Kentucky; his diocese extending from Kentucky to the Great Lakes, from the Alleghenies to the Mississippi. Flaget became highly influential in the councils of the U.S. church, and his various religious establishments included St. Thomas Seminary in 1812, the Sisters of Loretto and the Sisters of Charity of Nazareth in 1812 for the elementary education of girls, and St. Joseph and St. Mary's boys' colleges. He visited Rome in 1835 and, at the request of Pope Gregory XVI, toured France from 1837 to 1839. He retired in 1848 to ascetic solitude, practicing strict self-denial as a measure of spiritual discipline. The See, at his request, was moved to Louisville, where he is entombed in the Cathedral of the Assumption.

The new diocese was known as the "mother diocese" of the region west of the Allegheny Mountains. The new bishop at first refused the honor but was ordered to accept. His residence was a log cabin, which is still preserved at St. Thomas, near Bardstown. He began building the first cathedral west of the mountains at Bardstown in 1819. The See of this diocese was transferred to Louisville in 1841. Bishop Flaget consecrated Bishop Kenrick in 1830. Bishop Kenrick taught at Bardstown Seminary nine years and became Secretary to Bishop Flaget at the Second Vatican Council in 1829. He founded the *Catholic Herald* newspaper in 1833, and increased the number of churches from four to 94. (Today there are many *Catholic Herald* newspapers published in major Catholic centers around the world.) He established the Forty Hours Devotion in the United States in 1853. Dorothy received this information from Father Thomas T. McAvoy, former chairman of the department of history at the University of Notre Dame. Father McAvoy died in his office at the university library of a heart attack on July 7,

1969 (*Catholic Encyclopedia* Volume 5, viewed at the Kalamazoo, Michigan Public Library).

Four years after his ordination, the young Elisha Durbin went to the nearby seminary of St. Joseph at Bardstown, Kentucky, where in 1821-1822 he had as instructor Father Francis Patrick Kenrick, a distinguished theologian who later became Bishop of Philadelphia, Pennsylvania and Archbishop of Baltimore, Maryland. Before continuing with Father Durbin's story it may be useful to also examine the life of Francis Patrick Kenrick.

Francis Patrick Kenrick and Peter Richard Kenrick were Archbishops respectively of Baltimore, Maryland, and St. Louis, Missouri. They were sons of Thomas Kenrick and his wife Jane, and were born in the older part of the city of Dublin, Ireland, the first-named on 3 December 1797, and the second on 17 August 1806. An uncle, Father Richard Kenrick was for several years parish priest of St. Nicholas of Myra in the same city, and he cultivated carefully the quality of piety that he observed at an early age in both children.

Francis Patrick was sent by his uncle to a good classical school, and at the age of eighteen was selected as one of those who were to go to Rome to study for the priesthood. Here he became deeply impressed with the gentle bearing of Pius VII, who had just then been restored to his capital after long imprisonment by Napoleon Bonaparte, and the lesson it taught him bore fruit many years afterwards when he was called on to deal with the onslaughts on Catholics and their Church in the United States in the years of the Nativist and Know-Nothing uprisings. ("Know-Nothingism" will be covered later in this book.) His progress in his clerical studies was rapid, his sanctity conspicuous—so much so as to mark him out for early distinction. He confined himself to the study of his classbooks, lectures, and the study of the Scriptures, and worked out in his own mind not a few weighty problems. He soon acquired a familiarity with the patristic writings and the Sacred Text that enabled him later on to give the Church in the United States valuable treatises on theological and Biblical literature. He consulted no translations, but took the Hebrew text or the Greek, and pondered on its significance in the light of his own reason and erudition. The rector of Propaganda College, Cardinal Litta, had no hesitation in selecting him despite his youth, when a call came from Bishop Flaget for priests for the American field. He was chosen for the chair of theology at Bardstown Seminary, Kentucky (St. Thomas). This post he held for nine years while at the same time teaching Greek and history in the College of St. Joseph in the same state, and giving in addition professorial help in every educational institution in the state. He also did much valuable work in the missionary field, and engaged in controversy in the public press with some aggressive controversialists of the Episcopal and Presbyterian communions. He made many converts at that time, and in 1826 and 1827 had fifty to his credit, as well as a record of twelve hundred confirmations and six thousand communicants. His fame as a preacher was widespread, and his manner most winning.

In 1829 he attended the Provincial Council of Baltimore as theologian to Bishop Flaget, and was appointed secretary to the assembly. There, among the other weighty subjects, had to be considered the distracted state of the Diocese of Philadelphia, then laboring under the troubles begotten of the Hogan schism. Hogan was an excommunicated priest, who persisted in celebrating Mass and administering the sacraments despite the interdict, and had a considerable following in the city. Bishop Conwell had by this time become enfeebled and nearly blind, and Reverend William Matthews of Washington had been appointed vicar-general to assist him. Before the council rose it had named Father Kenrick as coadjutor bishop and forwarded the nomination to the Holy See. It was soon confirmed, Doctor Kenrick's title being Bishop of Arath *in partibus* (a Latin title conferred on non-residential or titular bishops). He was consecrated in Bardstown by Bishop Flaget, assisted by Bishops England, Conwell, David, and Fenwick, on June 6, 1830, being then only thirty-four years old. A quarrel with the trustees of St. Mary's broke out immediately on his arrival, resulting in an interdict being placed upon the church by the new bishop. This brought the trustees to their senses, and they gave up the contest for the control of the funds. They no longer had the power by means of which they had been using to browbeat the preceding ordinaries. Bishop Kenrick soon obtained the passage of a law to prevent the recurrence of such conflicts by having the bishop's name substituted for those of the trustees in all bequests for the Church. His first thought, after this trouble was over, was the erection of a seminary for the training of young men for the priesthood, the humble quarters in which he began the experiment eventually being succeeded by the present seminary of St. Charles Borromeo at Overbrook.

A terrible outbreak of cholera, the same outbreak that took the lives of three members of "Big Joe" Logsdon's family, took place in Philadelphia soon after the bishop's arrival, and he gained the gratitude of the authorities and the people at large for his exertions in the mitigation of the pest. He sent the Sisters of Charity to attend the stricken, and gave the parochial residence of St. Augustine's as a temporary hospital; the local priests, at the same time, went about fearlessly among the stricken, ministering to their spiritual comforts. For these services the mayor and councils of the city voted him public thanks. To the Sisters of Charity was tendered a service plate by the grateful authorities, but this offer was promptly and politely declined by those ladies. Soon after this episode Bishop Kenrick set about the utilization of the press for the spread of Catholic doctrine. He started the *Catholic Herald* placing the paper under the direction of the Reverend John Hughes, afterwards Archbishop of New York. He also began the erection of the Cathedral of St. John the Evangelist to replace St. Mary's, which had been so fruitful a source of trouble to him and his predecessor. Graver trouble soon started up in the form of the anti-Catholic Nativist outbreak of 1844. Furious mobs, maddened by inflammatory harangues about the Bible and the public schools, started out in Philadelphia, as in Boston and other cities, to attack churches and convents. They burned St. Augustine's in Philadelphia and attacked St. Michael's and St. John's, but were driven off by the military. They burned many houses in Kensington, the Catholic district, and killed many unoffending people, but were dispersed at length by the soldiers, leaving several of their number dead.

During this reign of terror, Bishop Kenrick did everything he could do to stem the rioting. He ordered the doors of all the churches to be closed and cessation of Divine worship as a protest against the boldness of the authorities, the clergy went about in ordinary civil attire, and the sacred vessels and vestments were taken from the churches to places of security with private families. These prudent measures had the effect of restoring a state of peace to the city. The Diocese of Philadelphia had earlier included Pittsburgh and a large part of New Jersey, and in 1843 it was divided, the Rev. Michael O'Connor being consecrated Bishop of Pittsburgh in August of that year by Cardinal Fransoni at St. Agatha's in Rome. This step proved a great relief to Bishop Kenrick, upon whom the care of his vast diocese and its arduous visitations at a period of primitive crudeness in traveling and accommodation, were beginning to leave a deep mark. In 1845 he visited Rome for the first time since his consecration and was received most graciously by the pope.

In August 1851, Bishop Kenrick was transferred to Baltimore as successor to Archbishop Eccleston, who had just died. Moreover, he received from the Holy See the dignity of Apostolic delegate, and in this capacity he convened and presided over the First Plenary Council of Baltimore in 1852. One of the results of that important gathering was the establishment of branches of the Society for the Propagation of the Faith. It was Archbishop Kenrick also who in 1853 introduced the Forty Hours' devotion into the United States. In 1854 he was called upon by the Holy Father to collect and forward to him the respective opinions of the American bishops on the doctrine of the Immaculate Conception. The latter part of the same year found him back in Rome as a participant in the ceremonies attendant on the proclamation of that dogma.

A fresh outbreak of anti-Catholic fury took place soon after the archbishop's return, occasioned by the arrival of Monsignor Bedini as papal nuncio, and the inflammatory and lying speeches of the ex-priest Alessandro Gavazzi, on the nuncio's action while in Bologna during the rising against Austria. (A "papal nuncio" is akin to a lawyer appointed by the pope to serve the Church in a civil government.) Many churches and convents were burned as in the previous outbreak, and many lives were lost in New England and Kentucky, in Cincinnati and other cities. But no religious disturbances occurred in Maryland to perturb the archbishop's closing years. The Civil War, however, soon came to rend his heart, and he died on the morning after the battle of Gettysburg, July 8, 1863, his end being hastened, it was believed, by rumors of the terrible slaughter that went on not far from his residence. When Bishop Kenrick went to Philadelphia in 1830 there were only four churches in the city and one in the suburbs, and ten priests, when he left in 1857, the diocese contained 94 churches and many religious institutions, and was the home of 101 priests and 46 seminarians, besides numerous religious orders. The chief literary works of Archbishop Kenrick were a new translation of the Bible, with a commentary; a "Moral and Dogmatic Theology;" a "Commentary on the Book of Job;" "The Primacy of Peter;" and letters to the Protestant bishops of the United States on Christian unity.

Six years of part time studies and part time labor passed, when Elisha John Durbin was ordained a Roman Catholic priest in 1822 (*Dictionary of Catholic Biography*, Delaney Tobin, Battle Creek, Michigan Public Library). Because he had not reached the canonical age for ordination, a dispensation had to be procured from Rome. Bishop David, who had been named Coadjutor of Bardstown in 1819, on September 21, 1822, ordained Elisha a priest, and for over a year his duties held him to St. Joseph's college and the cathedral church of the same name in Bardstown, Nelson County, Kentucky. In 1824 Father Durbin was entrusted with the pastoral care of the Catholic population of all of western and southwestern Kentucky with his headquarters near Morganfield, Union County. His pastoral jurisdiction covered thousands of miles of territory in every part where isolated Catholic families lived. After 1832 he was obliged in addition to visit Nashville, Tennessee at least once in the year in order to serve the Catholics there. He rode his missions on horseback. He always rode a white horse and appeared as a commanding figure whenever he was in the saddle.

Initially, the young priest took up his headquarters at Sacred Heart Church in Union County. After a short while, Father Durbin was assigned to St. Theresa's. Up to this time, priests in charge of Flint Island recorded the baptisms of the parish in the register of the church where they resided. Father Durbin began the register at St. Theresa's in March of 1824. On the first page he wrote,

> This book is designed to contain all the baptisms performed in the congregation of St. Theresa and all adjacent settlements from the mouth of Sinking Creek as high up as Hogback

Grove or James Hardesty's neighborhood and the town of Brandenburg.

During the seven years that he attended this mission, he baptized one hundred and sixty-two persons. His first entry reads as follows:

March 25, 1824, I baptized George, son of Wilfrid and Susan Greenwell. Born March 20, 1824. Godmother: Catherine Hunter.

According to pages 316 through 324 of the *History of Union County, Kentucky 1886*, Father Durbin's first assistant was Reverend Edward A. Clark in 1829. Father Durbin and Reverend Clark, who was ordained about 1829, served the mission of Union and the adjoining counties.

"*Let thy speech be better than silence, or be silent.*" (*Dionysius the Elder, 430-367 B.C.*) An anecdote is told of Father Durbin's first attempt at preaching, which is most likely true. In 1823, and for some time before and after that year, there was a no more generally known and respected non-Catholic citizen of Bardstown than General Joseph Lewis. He had fought for independence under Washington, but his patriarchal years sat lightly upon him, and he was at all times companionable, and often pleasantly jocular. Meeting the young priest on the street a half year after his ordination, the general addressed him: "Your people tell me, Durbin, that you can't preach. How comes that?" "I don't know whether I can or not," answered the cleric, with blushing modesty; and then he added, "I will know more about it on next Sunday, however, since I find that I have been booked for a sermon on that day." "If that is the case," said the old man, "I think I will be there to hear you."

It is believed that General Lewis also fought in the Civil War in the Kentucky Fifteenth Volunteer Infantry. It is recorded that Brigadier General Joseph Lewis' Kentucky Brigade, also known as the "Orphan Brigade" had occupied trenches while fighting in the Atlanta, Georgia area at New Hope Church, Pickett's Mill and Dallas in late May of 1864. The fight at Dallas on May 28th was the worst of the war for the Orphan Brigade, which did not receive word that an assault on the entrenched Federal forces had been cancelled. In their ill-fated attack, many Kentucky men who built the trenches became casualties just days after shoveling the dirt and placing the stones that still mark their position.

The general had not been in the habit of going to church anywhere, and it is presumed that Father Durbin had not much expectation of having him for a listener on the occasion of his initial discourse from the pulpit. But there he was, and in such a position that the young priest could not help but see him the moment he cast his eyes over the congregation. He got through with the reading of the Epistle and Gospel very credibly; and then he began to recite before his listeners his own thoughts, which had most likely been previously written out and memorized. For a dozen sentences or more there was no balk, but all at once he appeared to lose both himself and the thread of his discourse together. The pauses became longer, and the stammering greater; and at length, in a fit of desperation, he turned about and left the pulpit.

The next time General Lewis caught sight of the priest he hailed him and said,

> Except in one particular, Durbin, I cannot say much for your sermon of the other Sunday. You got along pretty pertly until your canoe got tangled in the bushes, and then you stuck! But there was one capital thing about it, nevertheless—it was short!

Father Durbin has never been considered an orator, neither by himself nor anybody else, but it would be a happy thing for the Church, here and elsewhere, if the preaching of those of her clergy who are acknowledged eloquent, were as productive of good results as has been the simple, heart-felt and easily understood pulpit utterances of Kentucky's patriarch priest (*The Centenary of Catholicity in Kentucky*).

Father Joseph Rogers, who succeeded the Reverend Charles J. Cissell as pastor of St. Anthony's Church in Breckinridge County, had turned the monastery building into a boys' school, himself being the principal teacher. Father Rogers was in failing health and had to surrender his pastorship by retiring. In these earlier years of his priesthood, following Father Rogers' retirement, Father Durbin visited the Breckinridge County missions as often as once a month.

Indeed, the pastor sent to the people of Union County in 1824, when they themselves were new to the country, a man who fully understood the grave responsibilities of his position. His zeal was unquestionable, and labor and fatigue and discomfort appeared as trifles when held against the spiritual welfare of others. Catholicism in Union County, and in all Southwestern Kentucky, is intimately connected with the name and personal labors of Reverend Elisha John Durbin, a venerable and most meritorious priest.

Before continuing with Father Durbin's life story, another story, about another cleric, should be told. While Father Durbin ministered to his fellow Kentuckians, a distant cousin, John Price Durbin, was a frontier clergyman too, but he was a Methodist.

Chapter 5

Methodist in the Midst

There was another Reverend Durbin we should mention in relation to Father Elisha John Durbin. Father Durbin's third cousin, one generation removed, was Reverend John Price Durbin, a minister in the Methodist Episcopal Church. He was given a license as a preacher on November 19, 1818.

In those early days of American history, there were not enough clergymen to minister to settlers. It should be noted that when Father Elisha John Durbin began his ministry in Kentucky, the women were Catholic, but the men were not. It was not uncommon for a Catholic to "abandon ship" if there were no priests to help meet their religious needs. They would instead affiliate with another religion. Perhaps this is why Reverend John Price Durbin became a Methodist when most of his ancestors were Catholic.

He was born near Paris, Kentucky in Bourbon County on October 10, 1800, about ten to twenty miles from where Father Elisha John Durbin was born earlier that same year. Reverend John Price Durbin was the eldest of five sons, and he became the father of five sons and two daughters, Augusta and Ann. He worked for a time as a cabinetmaker in Paris, Kentucky. When he was 13, his father died.

The pre-eminent preacher John Price Durbin entered western itinerary in 1818, but the name does not appear in any church Minutes until 1820. He was educated up to the 14th year, and was of the commonest kind of frontiersman. He worked for several years. Then, in the autumn of 1818 he converted to Methodism. (It is not known which religion he professed, if any, prior to 1818, but his grandparents were thought to be of the Protestand-Episcopal faith.) He felt the duty to preach the gospel and was appointed to the northwest corner of Ohio. Here he began his study in cabins, where there was but one room, which served as a chapel, parlor, kitchen, dining room, and chamber for the whole family. Reverend Durbin studied in winter by firelight, made by pine-knots and dry wood, prepared by boys who used to wonder at him as a living marvel (*History of M. E. Church* by Abel Stevens, LLD, page 494).

He began to study English grammar, and later Latin and Greek, through tutors and self-education. Durbin soon became a licensed preacher and in 1819 traveled to Ohio to begin his ministry. In 1821 he began to minister in Hamilton, Ohio, and at the same time took up studies at nearby Miami University. The following year he moved again and was forced to continue his studies independently.

The next year he was sent to Indiana with colleague James Collord who was later printer of the Methodist Book Concern, New York. At Collard's insistence he began to study English grammar. Toward the close of the year, Doctor Martin Ruter advised him to study Latin and Greek. The third year he was stationed in Hamilton, Ohio, twelve miles from Miami University at Oxford, Ohio. He went to the university on Monday, stayed all week, and returned on Friday evening to prepare for Sunday.

An act of the U.S. Congress in 1792 required that a university be established in the Miami River valley north of the Ohio River. Although the university was officially founded in 1809, instruction did not begin until 1824. Financial shortfalls forced Miami to close in 1873, but it reopened in 1885 with the support of the state of Ohio. Women were first admitted in 1888.

U.S. President Benjamin Harrison graduated from Miami University in 1852. William Holmes McGuffey was a faculty member from 1826 to 1836, during which time he created the first of his famous readers. The campus is the site of the McGuffey Museum, a national historic landmark.

Today, Miami University is consistently rated among the top national universities for teaching undergraduates. "The Public Ivys" by Richard Moll proclaims Miami one of eight public institutions most similar to the Ivy League schools for academic quality and collegiate atmosphere. Miami's focus is on undergraduate education. Students have one-on-one research opportunities with senior faculty, small seminar courses, and an unusually wide range of nearly 100 majors.

Following his studies at Miami, the next year he went to Cincinnati and was admitted to Cincinnati College with the personal countenance of Doctor Ruter and President Harrison. Graduating in 1825, he received simultaneous Bachelor's and Master's of Arts degrees. (*History of M. E. Church* by Abel Stevens, LLD, page 494).

Following graduation from Cincinnati College in 1825, he was appointed Professor of Languages at Augusta College, Kentucky. He married Frances B. Cook of Philadelphia on September 6, 1827. On December 19, 1831 John Price Durbin accepted a nomination to the Chaplaincy of the United States Senate. In 1832 he was chosen Professor of Natural Science in the Wesleyan University and in 1833 he became editor of the *Christian Advocate and Journal* in New York. For seven years he was the Itinerant Preacher of Indiana and Ohio.

(Cincinnati College traces its origins to 1819, the year of the founding of the Medical College of Ohio. In 1870, the City of Cincinnati established the University of Cincinnati, which later absorbed the earlier institutions. In 1906, the University of Cincinnati created the first cooperative education program in the United States through its College of Engineering. For many years, the University of Cincinnati was the second-oldest and second-largest municipal university in the country. In 1968, the University of Cincinnati became a "municipally-sponsored, state-affiliated" institution, entering a transitional period culminating on July 1, 1977 when the school became one of Ohio's state universities. The University of Cincinnati is today one of only 88 classified as a Research I University by the Carnegie Commission.)

John Price Durbin (1800-1876) was a Methodist minister elected head of the new administration of Dickinson College in Carlisle, Pennsylvania on June 7, 1833 (*Appleton Cyclopaedia of American Biography*, Volume II). At this point there was an amendment passed by the College to give the Presidency of the Board to the Principal of the College. Durbin was thirty-two years old at the time of his appointment. He had grown up quite poor in Kentucky, but went on to graduate from Cincinatti College in 1825.

On page 198 of *A History of Dickinson College* by Charles Coleman Sellers, as President of Dickinson College, Durbin was recognized as the first actual chief executive of the College. He went on to reopen the Grammar school and also established a Law Department.

Dickinson College originated as a grammar school that had been founded in 1773. At the urging of physician and political leader Benjamin Rush, it was chartered as a college in 1783 and was named for then-governor of Pennsylvania John Dickinson. Benjamin Latrobe, architect of the original U.S. Capitol in Washington D.C., designed the school's first permanent building which was completed in 1804. Two of the nation's oldest continuous literary societies, Belles Lettres (founded 1786) and Union Philosophical (1789), were founded at Dickinson. The college began admitting women in 1884. Notable alumni include Roger Brooke Taney, chief justice of the U.S. Supreme Court from 1836 to 1864, and James Buchanan, 15th president of the United States.

At Dickinson College, in the early 19th century, the dour traditionalism of President Atwater clashed with the Jeffersonian radicalism of Thomas Cooper, who made it possible for the college to purchase his late friend Joseph Priestley's scientific apparatus. Because of these controversies, Dickinson fell on hard times until 1834 when it came under the sponsorship of Methodists, regaining educational vitality through the leadership of its new president, John Price Durbin. During the Civil War, Dickinson sent her sons to fight on both sides, hopeful "that college loyalties would bind where civil strife separated."

In 1833, Dickinson College was approached by the Baltimore Conference of the Methodist Episcopal Church with an offer to incorporate the college under its direction. The Board of Trustees agreed, and control was transferred to the Methodist Church. Efforts were immediately made by the new Board to raise an endowment to support the institution, but the additional aid of state money was sought and gained to assist the rebirth of the College. A strong faculty was gathered, consisting of Methodist professors, with Durbin as President. In November 1836, construction was completed on a new building, East College, which provided space for recitation rooms as well as student living quarters. Also in 1836, Durbin purchased a building that was located across High Street that would come to be known as South College. Unfortunately, the original structure was completely destroyed by a fire in December of that year, and its reconstruction would not be completed until 1838. In 1842, Durbin began a tour of Europe and the Middle East, and he would later write two books on these travels. After his return, Durbin served another two years before he tendered his resignation to the Board of Trustees, explaining that he wished to return to the ministry. Around this same time, Durbin married Mary Cook, the sister of his first wife.

John Price Durbin was president of Dickinson College from 1834-1845.

He was responsible for establishing missions all over the world. Besides contributing to periodical literature, Doctor Durbin published *Observations in Europe, Principally in France and Great Britain* (two volumes, New York, 1844), and *Observations in Egypt, Palestine, Syria, and Asia Minor* (two volumes, 1845), and he edited, with notes, Wood's *Mosaic History of the Creation* (1831) (*Appleton Cyclopaedia of American Biography*, Volume II).

Some of his other works include the following. The substance of a Sermon in favor of aiding the Greeks in their present contest with the Ottoman power, delivered in the Presbyterian Church at Lebanon, Ohio, February 22, 1824; Inaugural address, delivered in Carlisle, September 10, 1834, upon the re-opening of Dickinson College; A letter to William H. Norris on the identity of fundamental doctrines in the Church of England, the Protestant Episcopal Church, and the Methodist Episcopal Church, 1844; *Unsere Mission in Deutschland*, in *Christlicher Apologete* 1850, 143; Pennsylvania Colonization Society, addresses delivered in the Hall of the House of Representatives, Harrisburg, Pennsylvania, April 6, 1852; James Burgh (1714-1775), *Rules for the Conduct of Life*, by James Burgh, to which is added, *The Proper Method of Preserving Health*, by Lewis Cornaro, with an introduction by J. P. Durbin, D.D., 1846.

In 1853, the General Anniversary of the Missionary Society of the M. E. Church was held in Buffalo at the Niagara Street Church, at a date that overlapped, in part, the date of the revival services held by Dr. Redfield. This would probably not have been done by a more experienced pastor. Possibly the difficulties that arose from this situation might have been avoided at that time if this conflict in date had not occurred. Bishop Janes, Abel Stevens, and John Price Durbin were among those present for the Anniversary occasion. One of those who preached was Dr. John Price Durbin, a leading light of those days, whom Dr. John A. Roche believed to illustrate more forcibly than any man he had known the greatest number of principles of homiletics (the art of preaching) and sacred oratory. Roberts was evidently not so deeply impressed, at least with that particular sermon, for in his Journal for January 23rd he wrote, "Dr. Durbin preached this morning from John 4:35 a clear intellectual discourse, wanting in spirituality and life." (Diary of B. T. Roberts, January 23, 1853. Quoted by B. H. Roberts, Benjamin Titus Roberts, page 71.) Bishop Edmund S. Janes, whose service as bishop of the Methodist Episcopal Church comprehended a generation, and whose "flute-like voice made upon the hearer a peculiar impression" also preached. Roberts could have said as the bishop did when he died, "I am not disappointed." Roberts characterized his discourse from Acts 9:31 as "rich in instruction and spiritual life." Above all, Roberts believed that the efforts made for the raising of money during this period in which "the aid of eloquence, and wit, and personal and church rivalry was invoked" dissipated the conviction that had been resting upon the people, and that when the revival meetings were resumed at the close of the Missionary Convention, they "found the wheels of the car of salvation were effectually blocked."

Reverend **JOHN PRICE DURBIN, D.D., LL.D.** (1800-1876)

After retirement from the college, Durbin began preaching in Philadelphia and in 1849 was elected presiding elder of the North Philadelphia area. In 1850 he was elected the Secretary of the Missionary Society, a position he would hold until 1872, when he was forced to retire for health reasons (*Appleton Cyclopaedia of American Biography*, Volume II).

He had held positions as pastor, presiding elder, professor and president of colleges, editor and author. He was small of stature and had a high voice. His preaching began with tone, look, and style to damp all favorable expectation were it not for his general fame. He excelled in illustration, picturesque, pathos (pity and compassion) (*History of M. E. Church* by Abel Stevens, LLD, page 494). He died in New York on October 17, 1876, and was buried in Laurel Hill Cemetery, 3822 Ridge Avenue, Philadelphia, Pennsylvania.

Laurel Hill Cemetery is in Fairmount Park. Its tombstones, monuments and mausoleums can be seen from Kelly Drive. A walk along its paths enables a person to see a vanishing piece of America—the Gothic, cluttered cemetery that is fast disappearing. The cemetery was planned as early as 1835.

Laurel Hill is truly a necropolis, a city of the dead, yet is situated in one of the most romantic spots in Philadelphia, overlooking Kelly Drive and the Schuylkill. There is a brooding air about it, probably caused by the crowded stones—it appears to be nearly filled—and it is situated almost hanging over the river. The monuments are distinctive at best, each one meant to outdo its neighbor in originality. In the last century Laurel Hill Cemetery was a place to promenade on a Sunday afternoon or a holiday. Strollers found it a favorite place for a ramble.

When the cemetery was opened, Charles Thomson, the secretary of the Continental Congress, had been resting quietly for 14 years in a cemetery at Harriton. The story is told that the promoters of Laurel Hill approached his heirs and asked to remove this distinguished American's body and his wife's to the new cemetery. The heirs, except for one nephew, refused. Soon after the refusal, grave robbers at Harriton were surprised at their task and threw the bodies they were robbing in a cart and beat a hasty retreat. These unfortunate bones were reinterred in Laurel Hill and a splendid monument to Thomson was erected over them. There is disagreement as to whether the bodies were those of Thomson and his wife, but the bones have remained undisturbed since under a handsome obelisk.

Laurel Hill is a treat for cemetery aficionados and history lovers alike. There, funerary art and history form a singular confluence. Other noted people are also buried there, such as the likes of the 18th century's Thomas Godfrey, who invented the mariner's quadrant, Thomas McKean 1734-1817, Signer of the Declaration of Independence, the 19th century's Henry Disston and locomotive powerhouse, Matthais Baldwin.

For more information on the remarkable Doctor Durbin, read the *Life of John Price Durbin, D.D., LL.D.* by James A. Roche, M.D., D.D., copyright 1889, New York, New York, Phillips and Hunt, Cincinnati: Cranston and Stowe. Here's what Lewis O. Brastow had to say about this book:

> The subject of this memoir was one of the most gifted preachers of the Methodist church of this country. The preparation of the memoir was evidently a work of love and is well worthy of the man whom it honors. We do not look for severe critical judgment, for excessive caution or reserve or for measured terms of praise. The author is an enthusiastic admirer and he pours forth his laudation without stint. Estimated by the severest literary standard it may be pronounced extravagant. The literary quality of the work is defective and at times distasteful.

> But we do not fail to catch much of the author's enthusiasm for the subject of his eulogy and we are constrained to rejoice and to be grateful that such preachers as Dr. Durbin are possible in an age like this and that the noble church that has done so much for this country is still able to produce them. One of the interesting and valuable features of the volume is its discussion of homiletical principles in the light of their concrete manifestation in the subject of this memoir. It in fact succeeds in becoming a valuable contribution to homiletical literature. It is to be cordially commended to students of homiletics as containing some of the most helpful and fruitful suggestions about preaching to be found. They are the more valuable that they interpret and generalize the concrete facts of Dr. Durbin's preaching.

Reverend John Price Durbin and Father Elisha John Durbin were two great men who were among America's pioneers in each their own way. Both men traveled extensively in performing God's work, however, Father Durbin's travels were far more rigorous, as we shall witness as we examine his nearly life-long ministry.

CHAPTER 6

▼

THE MINISTRY

To this point we have looked at the events and the people leading to the ministry years of Father Elisha John Durbin. To begin his ministry, in 1824 Father Durbin was given a parish which included one third of what is now Kentucky. For the next sixty-five years he covered a region consisting of a route of 11,000 miles on horseback (*Dictionary of Catholic Biography*, Delaney Tobin, Battle Creek, Michigan Public Library). Besides having earned for himself the title of *Patriarch Priest of Kentucky*, Father Durbin was also known as the *Apostle of Western Kentucky* (*Catholic Builders of Our Land*, Reverend John B. Ebel). Union County was the center of his mission. When Father Durbin reached the seat of his first mission, he found there a chapel of logs built upon the grounds of the Sisters of Charity of Nazareth at their establishment known then and still known as the Academy of St. Vincent (*The Centenary of* Catholicity in Kentucky). For several years Father Durbin served the mission alone. Its extent was from the Ohio River to Tennessee, and from the line of Jefferson County to the Mississippi. The points most visited by him, being central to considerable numbers of Catholic families, were Caseyville, in Union County; Flint Island, in Meade County; Fancy Farm, in Graves County; Knottsville and Panther Creek, in Daviess County; Paducah, in McCracken County; Henderson, in Henderson County; Bell's Mines, Marquette's and Dycusburg, in Crittendon County; Eddyville, in Lyon County; and Hardinsburg, in Breckinridge County. He erected churches. In the beginning, duty called him into Indiana and once a year to Nashville, Tennessee (*History of M. E. Church*, Abel Stevens, LL.D., page 494).

For a year after ordination, young Father Elisha John Durbin was stationed at St. Joseph's seminary and the Cathedral of the same name at Bardstown, where he assisted. Handicapped by extreme lack of self-confidence, he made little immediate impression on the people (Historical Tribute to St. Thomas Seminary, St. Louis, 1906). The following opens a window showing how this church, one of Father Durbin's first churches, was built.

St. Joseph Cathedral

St. Joseph Church is a magnificent structure. It began with the laying of its cornerstone in July 1816. Five years of hard work by its Bishop, Benedict Joseph Flaget, to raise enough money to begin the building, had preceded this historical day in the history of the Catholic Church in the United States. St. Joseph Proto-Cathedral is the first west of the Allegheny Mountains and is listed by the U.S. Library of Congress as a national landmark possessing exceptional interest and worthy of careful preservation. (The "Proto-" prefix has the meaning of being a first of its kind.) Having been sufficiently completed in 1819 for services to be held, it rose in the Kentucky wilderness as a monument to the faith, toil, and zeal, of the French priest, Benedict Joseph Flaget, who became the Bishop of the Diocese of Bardstown, and the families of the area, both Catholic and Protestant. It truly became a work of human hands. This historic edifice contains fine paintings and other gifts from Europe donated by Pope Leo XII, Francis 1, King of the Two Sicilies, and King Louis Phillippe of France, just to name a few.

In 1775, Catholic settlers, mostly of English and Irish descent, began emigrating chiefly from Maryland to Kentucky, an outpost of the crown colony of Virginia. The first missionaries came around 1787. In 1808 the four new Catholic dioceses, created at the request of Bishop Carroll of Baltimore, included Bardstown along with Boston, New York, and Philadelphia. The new diocese of Bardstown covered almost the entire Northwest Territory, south to New Orleans and as far north as Detroit.

In 1811, three years after he was appointed, Bishop Flaget arrived at Bardstown, traveling down the Ohio River by flatboat and overland from Louisville by wagon, accompanied by a group of seminarians. Bishop Flaget was able to build a small brick church near Bardstown, named St. Thomas. Soon he was consumed with the idea of erecting a cathedral of majestic proportions. Since most of the settlers were very poor, people contributed their materials and their labor as carpenters and masons to build the cathedral.

Architect and builder of the cathedral was John Rogers of Baltimore. Bricks were baked on the grounds, and solid tree trunks cut from the wilderness were lathed in a circular pattern to form the stately columns supporting the building.

The Cathedral was consecrated in 1819, though the interior was not fully completed until 1823. When the Episcopal See was moved forty miles away to the fast-growing city of Louisville in 1841, St. Joseph's became a parish church, hence, the title "proto-cathedral." In 1995 Bardstown was named a titular see by the Vatican for its contributions to Catholic Church heritage in America. Once again, Bardstown, only one of three titular dioceses in the U.S., has a bishop, though only in an honorary capacity.

The St. Joseph Proto-Cathedral complex, which includes Spalding Hall and Flaget Hall of what was originally St. Joseph College, is on the National Historic Register.

The people, in time, came to appreciate Father Durbin's single-hearted devotion to duty, his love of the ministry, and his constant labors in their behalf. Sometimes sporting a beard and a mustache, Father Durbin was only five feet, ten inches tall and weighed about 169 pounds. He attributed his surprising energy and good health, despite exposure to the elements, to simple foods and exercise from horseback riding (*The Catholic Advocate*, Louisville, 1836-1887).

In *A History of Sacred Heart Church*, Russellville, Kentucky, compiled by Father William M. McAtee for the parish's centennial observance to be held on April 29, 1973, a story of Father Durbin is told.

> Around 1830 Father Elisha J. Durbin was assigned to care for the Catholics of this area. His mission territory embraced the area now comprising the Diocese of Owensboro. In addition, he also made trips to Nashville until that diocese was formed in 1837, as well as trips into southern Illinois and Indiana. It has been estimated that during his sixty years as a missionary, this priest traveled over 500,000 miles from his headquarters in Union County, Kentucky, caring for Catholics throughout this vast area.
>
> During these years when few Catholics resided in southern Kentucky, we read that there were no Catholics in Logan County. Yet Father Durbin was known in the County; and when traveling through Russellville would be entertained at the

homes of prominent non-Catholics, such as Judge Ephraim Ewing, Elijah Hise or Thomas W. Stockdale.

The beginning of the construction on the railroad through southern Kentucky in the late 1850's was a boon to the growth of Bowling Green, Franklin and Russellville. Among the laborers arriving during that period were many Catholics directly from Ireland who were distressed at finding little opportunity of fulfilling their religious obligations.

(Ephraim B. Ewing was Missouri's state attorney general from 1856 to 1858. He died June 23, 1873. In 1858 Judge Ewing, then of Russellville, Kentucky, made a donation of a piece of property in Chicago to Cumberland University for the Theological School. It was a dead expense to the University until it was sold during President McDonnold's administration. The proceeds of the sale amounted to $12,000. When the property was first donated, the Ewing Professorship was established in the Theological School. About the time when Dr. McDonnold became president, the Trustees decided to buy, for $16,000, the Abram Caruthers property [later known as Divinity Hall] consisting of a large brick residence and sixty acres. They made a first payment, using a part of the building fund raised by Dr. T. C. Blake. This created some dissatisfaction, for the College of Arts was still without a permanent home. The Trustees then turned the property over to the College of Arts for its use. But there was still a mortgage on the property; and when it was about to be sold for $8,760, the balance due, the property was bought for the Theological School with $8,760 of the money received for the sale of the Ewing property in Chicago. The Theological School used the building, known as Divinity Hall, until 1896.)

(Elijah Hise [1802-1867] was born in Pennsylvania. He had been U.S. Charge d'Affaires to Guatemala in 1848; a member of the Kentucky state legislature; a state court judge; and a U.S. Representative from Kentucky's 3rd District from 1866 to 1867. He is interred at Maple Grove Cemetery; there's a cenotaph at the Congressional Cemetery, Washington, D.C. (A *cenotaph* is a tomb or monument erected in honor of a person whose remains are located elsewhere.) Hiseville, earlier called Blue Spring Grove, is an old town with an interesting past. It is located in the northeast corner of Barren County on Highway 70, which runs from the Mammoth Cave area, past Sulphur Well, the old health resort, and winds its way on into the mountains of eastern Kentucky. Hiseville had its statesmen, its doctors, its blacksmiths, and cobblers. The town also had its distilleries, where it is said the best wiskey and brandy could be purchased for 40 or 50 cents per gallon. In 1858, Hiseville organized its own State Guard Company. The first post office in the county located outside of Glasgow was established at Hiseville and went by the name of Blue Spring Grove for many years. Around 1867, the name was changed to Hiseville Post Office in honor of Elijah Hise, a native of the community, who at that time represented the district in Congress. It is said that Elijah Hise was a lawyer of great ability.)

One of Kentucky's early settlers, Francis Coomes, counted four priests in his list of descendants. His daughter Rachel married William Coomes of Owensboro, whose house was a station and resting place for Father Durbin and other priests in their visitations to that part of the State. Bishop David ordained Francis Coomes' grandson, Charles I. Coomes, a priest on 5 December 1830, and Fathers Durbin and Coomes were lifelong friends. Two weeks before his death, his ancient friend, Elisha J. Durbin, visited Father Coomes. The meeting between the two was so moving that it brought tears to the eyes of witnesses. If an angel of God had appeared at his bedside, the dying priest could not have exhibited more true joy.

Father Elisha Durbin's headquarters was near Morganfield, and his first assistant was Reverend Edward A. Clark, at St. Ambrose Church in Union County.

Father Durbin built churches, and it is likely that he performed much of the manual labor himself, as there were not many Catholic men around to give him a hand in those early days.

The first church he built was Sacred Heart of Jesus at St. Vincent, outside Waverly, in 1828, then the only Roman Catholic Church west of Breckenridge County and east of the Mississippi River. This was a simple rough log chapel. This church was dedicated on September 14, 1828. Either John F., or Robert Alvey, in favor of Bishop Flaget, made the deed for the property for the Sacred Heart church in 1818, and it was afterwards released by the heirs of the grantor in consideration of the sum of one dollar. The burial ground adjacent to the church is said to contain graves from this early period.

Then, in 1825 and 1826 he built St. Mary's Church, in Perry County on the Indiana side of the Ohio River. It was a small log building located approximately two miles from Flint Island, near St. Theresa parish in Meade County. This church was still in use in 1849.

Also in 1826 he built the second Church of St. Theresa in Meade County. (The first Church of St. Theresa was built in 1818 and stood in the lowlands near the river at Chenault.) The old section of the parish cemetery marks the site of the second church.

In 1828 he built the first church in Daviess County, St. Lawrence, a log church.

His next church project was St. Ambrose, also called the Lower Chapel, at Henshaw in Union County, built around 1833 on a grant of land from Thomas Cropper, of Virginia, of two hundred acres, and Father Durbin or his assistant attended it at the time, up to 1860, when it was transferred to the charge of the pastorate of St. Agnes' church in Uniontown.

He then built the first St. Jerome Church at Fancy Farm in Graves County in 1836. Its first resident pastor was Reverend Alfred Hogan in 1843, and the second assistant was Reverend Stephen Ward. After the pastor's death in 1848, it was served by Father Durbin himself or by Reverend Ward. Also in 1843 a post office was established with the name "Fancy Farm." Fancy Farm has a story and it is told later in this chapter.

He built St. Polycarp Church in Carmi, Illinois around 1847. Carmi lies on the East bank of the Little Wabash River in Southern Illinois. It was the Little Wabash that attracted the first settlers to the area in the period of 1809-1814.

In 1849 he built the first St. John the Evangelist Church in McCracken County.

Father Durbin built the Sacred Heart Church in Morganfield in 1855 to replace the original one, which had become inadequate for the large congregation. The Church of the Sacred Heart, costing $20,000 to build, was dedicated June 20, 1855. Upon the retirement of Father Durbin in 1873, Reverend T. J. Jenkins was appointed to the pastorship at Sacred Heart, in which he continued for sixteen months, and during which time he reorganized the congregation, established a school for boys, and built an addition to the rectory.

The Church of St. Agnes at Uniontown was built in 1860, the lot being donated by William David, a non-Catholic. Father Durbin was appointed pastor at St. Agnes. It was built across the street from the present-day Sanctuary. When a new St. Agnes church was built, it was on land donated by a non-Catholic. This church is still standing today.

St. Stephen Church at Smithland in Livingston County opened in 1860 and was located on the Ohio River at the mouth of the Cumberland. As the parish membership dwindled the building gradually fell into disuse and was demolished around 1870.

The first St. Louis Church, later renamed Holy Name Church, was dedicated at Henderson in 1861.

Father Durbin also built St. Francis de Sales Church in Paducah, Kentucky in 1864.

It is doubtful if history of missionary enterprise in the U.S. furnishes a parallel of continuous labor such as marked the career of Father Durbin—65 years a priest—200 miles a week on horseback—11,000 miles of territory to cover.

Father Durbin was given the care of western and southwestern Kentucky, about one-third of the state. Then he began a missionary career of over 60 years, hardly paralleled in the United States. For several years Father Durbin served the mission alone. Its extent was from the Ohio River to Tennessee, and from the line of Jefferson County to the Mississippi. The points most visited by him, being central to considerable numbers of Catholic families, were Caseyville in Union County; Flint Island, in Meade County; Fancy Farm in Graves County; Knottsville and Panther Creek in Daviess County; Paducah in McCracken County; Henderson in Henderson County; Bell's Mines, Marquettes and Dycusburg in Crittendon County; Eddyville in Lyon County; and Hardinsburg in Breckinridge County. When Father Durbin was appointed to the missions of Western Kentucky, the mission at Flint Island, St. Teresa's, became about as important as St. Anthony in Breckinridge and the Sacred Heart in Union County. In 1826, Father Durbin persuaded the congregation at Flint Island to put up a small log church. From 1824 to 1833, Father Durbin visited the Catholics of Daviess and McCracken Counties at long intervals. At Paducah, Father Durbin's mission became more and more important, and through his exertions, the first church of St. Francis de Sales was built there (*The Centenary of Catholicity in Kentucky*).

Minor stations served by Father Durbin were numerous. One of these was the house of Benedict Hardy, below Morganfield; one at James Woodward's, and afterwards at Mrs. Henrietta McAtee's, still farther removed in the same direction; one at Joseph Moore's, in Illinois, twenty-five miles below Shawneetown, and afterwards at John Lawler's, near the town named; one at Daniel McLaughlin's, opposite Flint Island, in the State of Indiana; one at Marcus Wathen's, below Uniontown; one at Allen Anderson's, in Webster county; and others at Benjamin Watkin's, Mrs. Wimsutt's, John Payne's, John Thompson's, and Benjamin Luckett's, in Union county. (Sister Anastasia, of the Nazareth community, was a daughter of Benjamin Luckett.) After 1832, Father Durbin was further charged with the stations at Franklin, Kentucky, and Nashville, Tennessee. The first named of these was at the house of Lawrence Finn, and the last at that of Philip Callaghan, in Nashville.

From his center in Union County he journeyed on horseback over his vast territory, erected churches, established stations, formed congregations, and visited isolated families. From constant exposure to the elements, his features had become marked. Father Durbin's ruddy complexion was once the occasion of a humorous incident. Jogging along the open highway one day, he raised his eyes from the page of his breviary from which he was reciting the canonical office, and perceived a stranger, also on horseback, approaching him from the opposite direction. When the two met, the priest bowed his head and was about to pass on; but he had not got two lengths of his horse away from the second rider when he was halted by the exclamation: "Halloo, stranger! You are just the man I have been looking for! Get off your horse for a minute and let me take a pull at your jug!" "My friend," said Father Durbin, who saw at once what the man was after, "I have no jug! I have no use for one, for I never drink spirits of any kind!" "No jug!" exclaimed the man incredulously; "do you mean to tell me that I don't know what sort of a bulge a jug makes at the bottom of a pair of saddle, bags!" Laughing at the oddity of the situation, the man having mistaken for a jug a bundle made up of a part of his priestly vestments—the priest replied: "You are altogether mistaken, sir! I have not about my person nor in my saddle bags as much as a drop of liquor of any kind; and furthermore, I spoke truthfully when I told you a bit ago that I am not in the habit of using spirits at any time or in any form." Looking at the priest intently for a full half minute, the man said at length: "Stranger, I hope you will not take offense at the remark, but if I were in your place, I would take in my sign!"

The Reverend Felix De Andreis CM, described conditions in the Kentucky missions of those days soon after arrival at St. Thomas, in Kentucky, November 22, 1816. Father De Andreis, another fabulous pioneer priest whose sanctity has led to consideration of his cause for beatification, in a letter home told how the frontier priest must be constantly on horseback winding his way along the trails among the thick woods, sometimes thirty to ninety miles to visit the sick or attend the various congregations. The churches, Father De Andreis noted, were constructed of logs, without ornamentation, and were scattered in the woods. At the churches on festival days both Catholics and Protestants gathered from twenty miles around. At those times the woods were filled with horses neighing as if a regiment of cavalry were in the vicinity.

The mass, sermon, confessions and baptisms on one of these visitations could take the whole day. Describing the country around St. Thomas, he said there were neither towns nor villages. Men, women, and children, of every age, came on horseback as far as fifteen miles to attend mass, and if they received communion sometimes had to remain fasting until they returned home in the evening (*The Catholic Advocate*, Louisville, 1836-1887).

Father Durbin's churches, stations and the rude homes of the poor were his only abiding places. Occasional communications from him appeared in the press but only in defense of truth or outraged justice. When he did write, it was cogently and elegantly (*Catholic Encyclopedia*, Volume 5, Newberry Library, Chicago, Illinois).

In those days of frontier hospitality, the priest on missionary trips was welcomed and given food and lodging by the planters, eager to receive visitors. Even Protestants would do all in their power to receive him well, though the best fare he could expect consisted of nothing but some very badly baked cornbread, salt pork, potatoes and water. This is the refreshment that the missionary finds after a long journey, having heard confessions the whole morning until one or two o'clock in the afternoon, said mass, preached, baptized, etc.; sometimes at five o'clock in the evening he is still fasting.

When Father Durbin was given charge of the Tennessee missions late in 1834 or early 1835, however, a brighter day dawned for the Catholics of the state. The little brick church in Nashville, unused since the time of Father Cosgrove, was in a dilapidated condition, and rather than put his parishioners to the expense of repairing it, Father Durbin offered mass in the homes of the people. Thus it is told that he "kept church" in the home of Philip Callagan.

Father Durbin would advertise his coming visits in articles in the press. Thus in the Catholic Advocate of August 6, 1836, he informs the Catholics of Tennessee that he will shortly visit the state. His present intention is to be in Nashville on the third Sunday in October. He will also visit Gallatin and Hartsville. Catholics residing in other parts of the state will please meet him in Nashville, or let him know, as soon as possible, their places of residence, that he may call on them.

In 1836, Father Elisha John Durbin was instrumental in establishing the first St. Jerome Church at Fancy Farm in Graves County, Kentucky. His chalice and paten from St. Mary's Parish, Shawneetown, Illinois, were used at the sesquicentennial homecoming Mass, April 13, 1836, at St. Jerome, Fancy Farm (*The Catholic Advocate*, Louisville, 1836-1887).

Fancy Farm is a Graves county town about eleven miles northwest of Mayfield. The town grew up around St. Jerome Church, built in 1836, and the first post office opened in 1843. The original St. Jerome's Church has been replaced with a more modern structure that sits on the original church site. The name of the town is said to have come from the well-tended farm of an early settler. Since 1880 Fancy Farm has been the home of the annual Fancy Farm Picnic. Held on the grounds of Fancy Farm Elementary School, formerly the St. Jerome Parish School, on the first Saturday in August, it has become a traditional venue for political campaigning. In the year 2000, they served over 18,000 pounds of barbecue.

In 1998, Patrick Crowley of The Cincinnati Enquirer formulated the following depiction of the Fancy Farm picnic at St. Jerome's.

The picnic gets more news coverage than any single political event in Kentucky. Above all Fancy Farm is known for two things: great food and loud, wild—and at times out-of-control politics. The political speaking attracts more news coverage than any single political event in the state. Reporters come from all of the major television markets and all of the state's major newspapers and radio stations are represented.

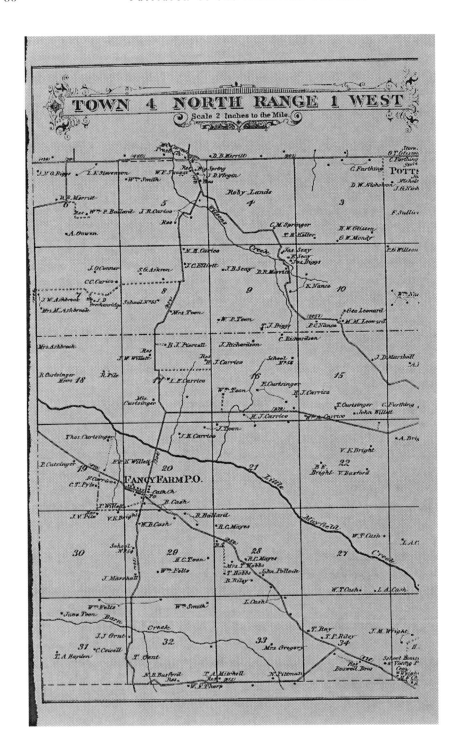

It is Kentucky's political equivalent of big time wrestling. The church picnic in far Western Kentucky has a century-long tradition of tangy barbecue and saucy campaigning.

The Fancy Farm picnic at St. Jerome's Catholic Church in Graves County began 119 years ago as a reunion for the members of the small country parish. Proceeds are used to help fund school and community projects. It soon evolved into a political event as well. Every first Saturday in August, it becomes the epicenter of Kentucky politics and launch pad for the autumn campaign season.

It has long been known for its humorous stump speeches, biting barbs and funny, yet sometimes nasty, exchanges between candidates and their opponents' supporters. All of Kentucky's elected officials are usually scheduled to attend and speak. It also serves as the kickoff for the fall election campaigns. In modern picnics, efforts were made to attract one or all of the United States presidential candidates.

During one governor's race, things got out of hand when busloads of partisans used noisemakers, vicious heckling, props and hurled objects to disrupt the speakers. Ever since, the picnic's organizers have tried to quell some of the venom. One of the people affiliated with the event implored the crowd Saturday not to use artificial noisemakers, large signs or heckling. The object is to get under a politician's skin, and many of the gimmicks and comments seem to do the trick.

The picnic each year attracts more than 10,000 people. While the 2:00 p.m. political speaking is a major drawing card, people with Graves County and Fancy Farm roots traditionally return for the annual event. Many families use it as an annual homecoming celebration.

The eating starts Friday night with a huge fish fry at the Knights of Columbus Hall on the church grounds. Saturday, more than 20,000 pounds of pork and mutton barbecue are hickory grilled in long cement pits, and then served as sandwiches or as part of a buffet feast that includes fried chicken, fresh grown vegetables, steaming casseroles and homemade desserts.

The politicking begins about 1 p.m., when Democrats and Republicans stake their spots around the stage where candidates will at least try to deliver fiery, often humorous and sometimes nasty stump speeches. At 2 p.m. the speaking commences, and so does the noise as the crowds taunt, mock and try to shout down the politicians. Most years both parties bus in dozens of vocal young people and college students who delight in disrupting the speeches.

Since then picnic organizers have instituted rules that eliminated most physical contact and air horns. And the area just in front of the speakers' stage is roped off to keep the crowd at bay. But the heckling hasn't subsided. It's still a mainstay of the picnic.

The following article was copied from The Western Watchman—April 9, 1887—St. Louis, Missouri.

> REVEREND ELISHA J. DURBIN—DEATH—LIFE SKETCH DEATH CLAIMS REVEREND ELISHA J. DURBIN After a long and useful life for sixty-five years in the service of the Lord.
>
> We have to record our loss, the loss of the beloved, venerable and self-sacrificing priest. To us have come the loss; to him, arrived the time for eternal reward. The old ties; binding us in the lives of our citizens to the birth of our century are rapidly, by death, being severed, and now but few, and very few, remain. We desire to give a brief, and we regret necessarily, imperfect notice of the early life and sacerdotal career of the venerated deceased.
>
> Continuous exercise in manual labor inured him whilst yet in early youth to the endurance of great and prolonged strain on his physical powers. He eagerly grasped the limited educational advantages afforded where he was brought up, and we learn throughout his stay under the paternal roof of his unselfishness, docility and obedience.
>
> We know how the fateful revolution in France wracked many a school of theology, and desecrated many a shrine; how the saintly Benedict J. Flaget (afterwards our first bishop), with others, left his native land for the cause of the faith, reached Baltimore, and with the pious Fathers David and Badin, in a floatboat, descended the Ohio to the falls; it is perhaps needless to recall, "that flatboat was at once the cradle of the seminary and the Church in Kentucky." Our noble Cathedral is a fitting monument to Bishop Flaget.
>
> Father Badin is remembered as the Apostle of Kentucky, and the first seminary within its limits arose under the eye of that illustrious Sulpician, Father David, who afterwards, in 1819, was consecrated Bishop of Mauricastro. To this first seminary, cradled in the flatboat on the Ohio, we find John Durbin and his wife in 1816, at his earnest solicitations, take their pious son Elisha. He was impelled to the Seminary of St. Thomas by a vocation from above.

The course in the seminary presented no holiday time to the young Levites. Half their hours were devoted to study, the other half to the labors in the field, the duties of the workshop, or to such other toil called for by needs of the institution. The discipline was rigid, food plain and drink unvaryingly water.

The young Elisha was undepressed by the difficulties of study; there was in his spirit an ever-renewing spring impelling him forward; it was not his to falter or look behind. For six years he remained at the Seminary, and on the twenty-first day of September 1822 the region was placed beneath his pastoral charge. Let us look at it on the map. On the one side, the Ohio, on another, Tennessee, on the east the western line of the county of Jefferson, and on the west the Mississippi. This territory lay within his charge, but it did not limit the domain of his spiritual stewardship. Across the Ohio it was his to attend the Catholics of Illinois, and for many a season, in addition, had he to minister to the faithful, then few, at Nashville, Tenn., and this all unaided and all alone, for many a year.

Providence fits men for the exigencies which arise and the necessities which they are to meet.

Through the countless square miles the sphere of Father Durbin embraced lay scattered hamlets inhabited by professors of the faith. Here and there isolated individual Catholics were stationed long, long miles apart, whilst in many places, roads were but a dream of the future, not advanced enough to be a hope, and often danger lay along the course.

These, all these, in every sorrow, in the loosening of the chains of the penitent, in breaking the Bread of Life, in the regenerating of the newest come to earth, or composing and absolving the departing, and in the need of every priestly care were ministered to by Father Durbin, as we have said before, unaided and all alone.

His center of operations, so to speak, was at Morganfield, Union county, Ky. How did he perform the duty? Almost ever on horseback, from long before dawn until long after day had done, and sometimes far into the night. He crossed the Ohio in every kind of weather, in frail boats; his hours of sleep took but little from his hours of action, and they were irregularly and fitfully enjoyed. He was undeterred by fiercest blizzard, and unstayed by treacherous snow-wreath, and the nipping frost left his energies uncontrolled.

He was undiscouraged by length of travel, where the path lay lost, or where intervening distances precluded refreshment or repose. The sacred call of duty was sounded, it was ever responded to; nor was Father Durbin ever reluctant, or tardy, or aught but joyous in the performance of its behests. His journeys on horse-back never told less than two hundred miles a week. Absolute rest he had none. His resting time was spent in the confessionals in the celebration of the Holy Sacrifices in the various duties which make demands upon a priest, and in collecting means, and in striving and endeavoring to erect fitting temples for the worship of God.

In physique, he was a man above the middle stature, lithe, and vigorous of frame. In early years he was of pleasant manner and appearance, but long exposure to inclemencies of weather, had tanned his complexion, and almost gnarled his features.

As a preacher, the Reverend Father would not have been classed high among the schools where tawdry eloquence, garish sensuousness and kaleidoscopic doctrine obtain honor, but he was pervaded with the apostolic spirit and his doctrine according to the Rock of Peter, had been impressed indelibly upon his youthful mind by the lectures of that eminent theologian, Bishop David, and he had at all times reason for the faith that was in him.

As we have mentioned, his residence was at Morganfield. There in the year 1820, the Community of the Sisters of Charity of Nazareth, had founded the Academy of St. Vincent. On their grounds they erected a log hut chapel. It was the only place, on the arrival of Father Durbin, to offer up the Divine Sacrifice. He at once girded himself to the holy work, but relaxed not a moment of his other labors, he girded himself to erect a fitting temple. It rose beneath his care, and stood close by the site of the old log chapel on the grounds of the

Sisters of Charity. It was dedicated to the Sacred Heart. In the year 1828, on the fourteenth day of September, the anniversary of the Exaltation of the Holy Cross, it was blessed by the Right Rev. Benedict J. Flaget, then Bishop of Bardstown. It was blessed when the Rev. Father had reached the 28th year of his age, and the sixth of his ordination.

The Catholic population of the district had increased, and required more visitation, and spiritual succor was needed in places where Catholics had not been before. Still his round of duties was the same.

He afterwards set his heart on building a church at Fancy Farm, in Graves county. He strove with hope to build it, his energy was crowned with success and he saw it blessed under the invocation of St. Jerome, in the year 1836.

In the course of time, the flock, small upon his arrival at Morganfield, and which had increased rapidly up to the building of the church in 1828, had so further increased in numbers as to need a more spacious edifice than that which succeeded the log hut chapel.

A new church of adequate dimensions was erected through the incessant efforts of Father Durbin. He loved his people, was affable to everyone, and approachable by all. His sternness was exhibited only in the demands he made upon his own powers and physical frame. His remembrance of faces was extraordinary; he knew every member of his flock personally, and had ever the cheerful and kindly greeting.

No surprise then, that all reverenced and loved him. No surprise, that all reverence and respect were wielded spontaneously to him by those without the fold. Amidst the pioneers of his great districts he watched and prayed for fifty years. Even when having passed the allotted times and the almost superhuman efforts began to tell on his human strength, he strove gallantly to keep up the good work.

His Ordinary heard of his over-tasked strength, and knowing that there is a time for all things, wrote to Father Durbin that for him it should be now. The Bishop wished that he would stay at the Cathedral in our city, but the Father, as Elisha of old was unwilling to lay aside the works upon the performance of which he had set his heart.

He grew feeble and still more feeble in frame. At length it was recognized that he should relinquish his beloved parish which he had served so long and so well. He received instead the parochial charge of the Catholics at Princeton, Ky. There was at that time a line of rail from Elizabethtown to Paducah. Growing weaker still, at the request of his Bishop, he retired from active life, and decided to spend his remaining years at St. Joseph's College, Bardstown, close by the church where he was ordained past fifty years gone by, and which college was rich to him in memories of the first years of his priesthood. But for him, no more than there had been for St. Alphonsus, there was no time for idleness upon earth. He besought his Ordinary to be permitted to go once more into active duty. His Bishop did know how to refuse the glowing fervor in the aged priest.

We see him assigned to the chaplaincy of the Hospital of Sts. Mary and Elizabeth in our city. Leaving there we see him where he wrought his last work in the vineyard of the Master, chaplain at Shelbyville, Kentucky, Our Lady of the Angels Convent, in charge of a Community of Francescan Sisters. A chaplain within the limits of that great territory where once he had served alone.

He continued to the last to celebrate the Holy Sacrifices though his strength was fading fast. On the 19th of March he wrote to his Bishop, 'that the communicants were now obliged to approach him on the platform close to the altar, as his weakness prevented his going down the steps.' The Bishop stated during the burial service, 'that day he was dead.' He died at Shelbyville.

The following article appeared in The Messenger (a newspaper) on Friday, January 4, 1985, and was found in the Archives of Mount St. Joseph, Maple Mount, Kentucky 42356 by Lucille Lawler

Today, southeastern Illinois is a stronghold of Catholic faith, but 180 years ago, there was no one of the faith living in this area. In 1819, John and Elizabeth Lawler arrived at Shawneetown with their son, Michael Kelly. They were followed by former neighbors and friends from Ireland and established the nucleus of the Catholic Church in the five county area.

Ties to Kentucky

These faithful Catholics were concerned because the nearest priests lived in Kaskaskia, Ill. and Vincennes, Ind. After a few years of praying and looking for a pastor, a young priest on horseback arrived at the clearing in front of the Lawler cabin in May 1824. He told them that he had come to serve them. This young priest was Father Elisha John Durbin from St. Vincent, Ky. He had been ordained just two years earlier at Bardstown, Ky.

This patriarch priest of Kentucky came from a long line of hardy ancestry. A relative of the pioneer priest, Ross Durbin who lives in St. Louis, has traced the family genealogy back to Samuel Durbin, who was born in 1698 and to Ann Logsdon, who was born around 1703. Elisha John Durbin was born on Feb. 1, 1800, in Madison County, Ky., to John D. Durbin and Patience Logsdon Durbin. His parents were natives of Baltimore, Md.

While the Logsdons of Kentucky were reported to be of large stature, Father Durbin was only five feet, ten inches tall and weighed about 160 pounds. He attributed his surprising energy and good health, despite exposure to the elements, to simple foods and exercise from horseback riding.

After completion of studies at St. Thomas Seminary, Bardstown, Ky., Elisha Durbin was ordained on Sept. 21, 1822. Two years later, Father Durbin was entrusted with the care of the entire population of southeastern Illinois, western and southwestern Kentucky and southern Indiana. His pastoral jurisdiction covered thousands of miles of territory where isolated Catholic families lived. His "parish" was extended in 1832 to include an annual visit to Nashville, Tenn.

Vast, Wilderness Parish

These many miles were traveled in good and bad weather on horseback. A priest friend calculated that Father Durbin's combined journeys during his 62 years in the priesthood would be underestimated at 500,000 miles.

The newly-appointed circuit-rider priest made his headquarters at St. Vincent, Ky., home of the Sisters of Charity of Nazareth. When Father Durbin first arrived at St. Vincent, there was a small log church. Within two years of his arrival, Father Durbin was able to point with pride to two churches that he was instrumental in erecting: a new one at St. Vincent near the site of the log church and a second one at St. Ambrose in Union County, Ky.

Eventually, the Sisters at St. Vincent expanded their institution which grew into an outstanding girls' school. Many families from southern Illinois as well as from Indiana and Kentucky sent their daughters to this school. It was a place of higher education where Catholics and non-Catholics alike could learn music, art, stitchery and religion.

Ministry in Southern Illinois

Records show that Father Durbin began his pastoral ministry in the present Belleville Diocese in May 1824 with the baptism of Margaret Lawler, the four-year-old daughter of John and Elizabeth Lawler. In September of the same year, three children of area families were baptized by Father Durbin, according to early church records kept at St. Vincent. Separate records were opened for the Illinois parishes in 1842. These children, John Milney, Edward Mattingly and Peter Sanders, were from two to five-years-old, leading us to believe that no priest had been in the area for baptism for at least three or four years.

In his Memoirs, written after his service in the Civil War, Gen. Michael Kelly Lawler left the following comments about the young Father Durbin:

To the Catholics eager to learn of the next visit of Father Durbin, the message of his coming brought cheer and great preparations—Oxen were put to the yoke and family readied for a three-day visit, the one the day before Father Durbin's arrival and the day after the services.

The children must have loved going to Mass as it was a holiday, although there were no schools to close. Parents provided both academic and religious instruction in their homes in the early 1820's and 1830's. The people's love for the missionary is evident in their nickname for him: "Daddy Durbin."

While riding this circuit, it was Father Durbin's custom to carry the sacred vessels and vestments for Mass in his saddle bags. In The *Centennary of Catholicity in Kentucky*, written by Hon. Ben. J. Webb and published in 1884, a story is related how Father Durbin's bulging saddle bags and florid complexion was once the occasion of a humorous incident.

Riding along the road one day, Father Durbin raised his eyes from the pages of his breviary to greet a stranger who had stopped his horse to visit for a moment.

Looking for a Jug

"Halloo, stranger! You are just the man I'm looking for. Give me a swig from your jug," the traveler said to the priest. "My friend," Father Durbin replied, "I have no jug nor do I have use for one. I do not drink."

"No jug! Then what sort of bulge is that in your saddle bags?" the stranger challenged the missionary. "I told you the truth the first time, I have no spirits at any time," Father Durbin said.

The man looked intently at the priest's red face and nose and the bulges in the saddle bags for a full half minute and rode away saying, "If I were in your place, then, I'd take in my sign."

Establishing the Church

Father Durbin may have endured many hours in the saddle, but he lived to see the fruits of his labors establishing the Church in southern Illinois. The first church built in Gallatin County was at Waltonboro or Pond Settlement. Built in honor of St. Patrick in 1853, it grew from the early visits of "Daddy Durbin."

This was a small log structure with most primitive furnishings; split logs with sticks for support served as pews. The poverty of the church reflected the poverty of the parishioners. For example, shoes were so rare that they were carried under the worshippers' arms until they reached the church door at which time they were slipped on.

Missions in White County

Thirty miles north of St. Patrick's was another Irish town, known as Dolan Settlement or Enfield. Patrick Dolan was possibly the first Catholic in White County and was there to welcome Father Durbin. By 1847, the town of Carmi had its first Mass said by Father Durbin in the home of John and Catherine Rebstock, natives of Baden, Germany. Their home became a shrine for worship when Father Durbin came to that corner of White County.

In 1841, Father Durbin started visiting the Catholics at Auxier Prairie in the neighborhood of Piopolis. A number of families from Ersinger and Bilsenger, Baden, Germany, had sailed for 41 days to New York City, from which they traveled to Pittsburgh where they took flatboats down the Ohio to Shawneetown. Led by John Leonard and Cajetan Aydt who had come earlier to scout for good land, they decided to build their homes on land which today comprises the parish of St. John the Baptist, Piopolis. Father Durbin was the first priest to visit and celebrated the first Mass in the log cabin of Nicholas Engel.

Other parishes in southeastern Illinois, including Equality, Metropolis, McLeansboro and Olney as well as parishes in western Kentucky were fortunate to have Father Durbin minister there during their early years. Catholics in many local parishes no doubt have signatures of this venerable priest in their early records. St. Mary Church, Shawneetown, has relics of this pioneer priest including his monstrance, chalice, paten and altar stone, which was used when Father said Mass in the home of Mary Handmore.

Less Than Eloquent Homilist

A story is also told about Father Durbin lest one is led to believe that he received only praise while ministering to his scattered flock in three states. Father Durbin was not perfect and his people admitted that he could not preach. During his first year at Bardstown, he would memorize his sermon, then proceed to forget his lines, stammer, stop and at times just walk away from the pulpit.

He never was considered an orator, but it would be a happy day for the Church if its clergy were as productive of good results as this simple, heart-felt, grace-filled Elisha Durbin of pioneer days.

The Final Years

Although St. Mary Parish, Shawneetown, received its first resident pastor in 1847, Father Durbin's signature can be found in parish records until 1859. At age 73, Father Durbin was released of his pastoral duties in Union County, Ky., but the aged missionary continued to minister to Catholics living along a route from Elizabethtown to Paducah, Ky. He finally retired to the College of St. Joseph, Bardstown, where he was surrounded with much care and love until he passed away in his 87th year.

About the Author—Mrs. Lucille Lawler is a substitute teacher, historian and devotee of Father Elisha Durbin. She and her husband, James, of Ridgway, have six children and seventeen grandchildren.

This article includes a photograph with the following caption. "Durbin Relics—Sacred vessels, which Father Elisha Durbin once carried in his saddle bags and used as he ministered to Catholics scattered across the southern Illinois frontier, are now property of St. Mary Parish, Shawneetown. Pictured are "Daddy" Durbin's monstrance, chalice, paten and altar stone.

Following is another article that appeared in the Mayfield (Kentucky) Messenger newspaper on March 22, 1987.

"Daddy" Durbin died 100 years ago

Horseback priest

By Wendell Givens

Messenger Staff Writer

He was affectionately known among some of his parishioners as "Daddy" Durbin and other members of his congregations in three states admitted 'he couldn't preach.'

But the "Priest on Horseback" is remembered as one of Kentucky's most accomplished and revered ministers.

At the time of Reverend Elisha J. Durbin's death in March 1887, at a convent at Shelbyville, Kentucky, at age 87, he was the second-oldest priest in the nation.

St. Jerome Catholic Church in Fancy Farm is one of ten churches which Father Durbin is credited with helping to found.

Members of the Fancy Farm church acknowledged the 100th anniversary of Father Durbin's death during services on Sunday.

"Because we are in the Season of Lent, while we're not celebrating this anniversary, we are acknowledging the 100th anniversary of Father Durbin's death and remembering with deep gratitude the gift of his services to our community," according to Sister Mary Lunardi of St. Jerome Church.

St. Jerome's present Pastor, Father Jerry Riney, shared some private thoughts about the founder of the Fancy Farm church.

"Last year as we celebrated the 150th year of our parish, Father Durbin's name was mentioned often. On April 13th of last year, we used Father Durbin's chalice and paten in our service. During that time a historical marker in front of our church was dedicated to the parish and Father Durbin," according to Father Riney.

"His pioneering missionary spirit, his religious courage to blaze trails of Catholicity in West Kentucky and throughout a wide area edify anyone familiar with Father Durbin's life," Rev. Riney continued.

"What vision spurred Father Durbin? It had to be his vision of Church, his love for the faith. Today, we who stand upon the shoulders of such great men as Elisha Durbin are continuing that same vision.

"We're challenged to let our faith be active and to reach deep into roots of our history. Faith must be chosen as a commitment and it must be internalized for it to take on meaning in today's society," Father Riney concluded.

Widely recognized as one of the pioneer priests in Kentucky, Father Durbin spent 65 years in religious service to thousands of Catholics in near-frontier settlements in parts of West Kentucky, West Tennessee and Southern Illinois.

During his ministry from September 1822, until his death on March 22, 1887, Father Durbin was instrumental in founding the following churches:

Saint Mary Church in Perry County, Indiana, in 1825; the second church of St. Teresa in Meade County in 1826; the first St. Lawrence Church in Daviess County in 1828; the second Church of the Sacred Heart at St. Vincent in 1828; St. Ambrose Church in Henshaw in 1833; St. Jerome Church in Fancy Farm in 1836; St. Francis de Sales church in Paducah and St. John the Evangelist Church in McCracken county in 1849; St. Stephen church in Smithland in 1860; St. Louis (later Holy Name) Church in Henderson in 1861.

During most of his 65-year ministry, the native Kentuckian traveled by horseback to backwoods settlements along his 150-mile circuit in four states.

Father Durbin was born February 1, 1800, in Madison County, Kentucky, to parents who were natives of Baltimore.

Following completion of studies at St. Thomas Seminary in Bardstown, young Durbin was ordained in September, 1822.

"There is a tradition that he began his studies for the priesthood at Dominican College of St. Thomas, St. Rose in

Washington County," according to a historical tract written by Rev. John Lyons of Louisville.

But finding that his vocation was not with the order of Preachers he entered the diocesan seminary at St. Thomas in Nelson County when he was 16 years old.

His theology was completed at St. Joseph's Seminary, Bardstown, and he was ordained with dispensation because of age, in St. Joseph Cathedral on Sept. 21, 1822.

After serving as teacher in St. Joseph College and assistant at the Cathedral until March 1824, Father Durbin began his long and eventful labors in Western Kentucky, according to Rev. Lyons' writings.

Father Durbin took up headquarters in Sacred Heart Church in Union County and from there he began attending missions from Union County to the Mississippi River in extreme West Kentucky and beyond.

His circuit-riding duties allow the young priest to visit small, isolated pockets of Catholics in Southern Indiana and Illinois and, beginning April 1832, he began periodic visits in West Tennessee and as far east as Nashville.

For years, Father Durbin traveled on horseback along the lonely, winding roads and trails in his three-state circuit.

Finally, help came with the appointment of assistants and resident pastors in the larger settlements and, with their aid, more parishes were established and churches erected, according to Rev. Lyons' research paper.

The fact of Father Durbin's withdrawal early in life from the order of Preachers might have been the result of self-examination by the budding priest.

According to facts compiled by writer Lucille Lawler in Belleville, Illinois, the good priest "was not a preacher."

"A story is told about Father Durbin lest one is led to believe that he received only praise while ministering to his scattered flock in three states," writer Lawler said.

"Father Durbin was not perfect and his people admitted that he could not preach. During his first year at Bardstown, he would memorize his sermon, then proceed to forget his lines, stammer, stop and at times just walk away from the pulpit," Ms. Lawler wrote.

But the minister found his natural environment in the saddle, in backwoods towns and cabins along his circuit and among children of parishioners.

Father Durbin's arrival in one outlying section of his 150-mile circuit might have been typical in hundreds of other communities, including Fancy Farm.

No other person of Catholic faith lived in Shawneetown, Illinois, where John and Elizabeth Lawler and son, Michael, arrived in the Southern Illinois settlement in 1819.

After several years of searching for a Pastor, 'A young priest on horse arrived at the clearing in front of the Lawler cabin in May 1824. He told them he had come to serve them. This young priest was Father Elisha John Durbin from St. Vincent, Kentucky...' according to Ms. Lawler's writings.

During his 62 years in the priesthood, Father Durbin's combined journeys on horseback totaled more than 500,000 miles, according to another researcher.

His home-base at St. Vincent in Union County, Kentucky, also was the home of the Sisters of Charity of Nazareth.

When Father Durbin arrived at St. Vincent there was a small log Church. Within two years, the young priest was instrumental in building two other churches there. Eventually, the Sisters at St. Vincent extended their institution into the outstanding girls' school.

Many families from Southern Illinois and Indiana and West Kentucky sent their daughters to this school. It was a place of higher education where Catholics and non-Catholics could learn music, art, stitchery and religion.

The priest always had an affinity for children and their need for education, according to all his biographers.

Shortly after the end of the Civil War, writer Michael Kelly Lawler compiled the following notes concerning Father Durbin's image among parishioners in Southern Illinois:

"To Catholics eager to learn of the next visit of Father Durbin, the message of his coming brought cheer and great preparations...Oxen were put to the yoke and family readied for a three-day visit, the one the day before Father Durbin's arrival and the day after the services."

The parishioners and their children's affection for the young priest was evident in their nickname for him: 'Daddy Durbin.' Following establishment of churches, the young priest always made sure the congregation attended to educational needs of their children.

In varying degrees, the same "church-then-school" pattern was followed in most communities where the horse-riding priest established churches, including Fancy Farm in Graves County.

Following establishment of the first St. Jerome Church Fancy Farm in 1836, the parish eventually built parochial schools which for years drew Catholic and non-Catholics students from several surrounding communities.

Even as recently as 1949, under the pastorship of Rev. Edward Russell, Fancy Farm parishioners completed one of the most modern new schools in Graves County at that time. The school has been remodeled and expanded even more since that time.

Originally the new Fancy Farm school housed six classrooms, a library, a gymnasium-auditorium and it was built for a cost of $90,000 cash—a unique bargain even 38 years ago.

Although the Fancy Farm school became part of the state public school system in 1933, every penny of construction costs of the new school in 1949 came from parishioners, in addition to volunteer labor.

After merger with the public school system in 1933 during the Depression, members of the sisters of Charity of Nazareth continued to teach at the school until the first public school teacher joined the Fancy Farm faculty about 1951.

In addition to education improvements, the Fancy Farm community erected its present church in 1895, the third church to serve the community since the log structure erected during Father Durbin's ministry in the early 1800s.

Father Durbin's ruddy face and rather small 5-10, 160-pound frame belied his tremendous inner strength encourage. However, more than 60 years of lonely, backwoods ministry eventually took its toll.

Following development of West Kentucky parishes, nearly all churches erected by the old priest had obtained resident pastors. By 1872, his mission territory had been reduced to that section of Kentucky lying between the Tidewater and Tennessee Rivers.

Early in 1873, Father Durbin resigned his pastorate at Sacred Heart to devote full time to his remaining missions. Taking up headquarters in Princeton, where he purchased property for a church, he served Catholics scattered throughout Caldwell, Livingston, Crittenden, Lyon and Trigg counties for the next eight years.

"Then in 1881 in the old priest's 81st year, Bishop McCloskey removed the zealous old priest from the hardships of the missions and appointed him chaplain at St. Vincent Academy in Union County," according to writings by Rev. Lyons.

But retirement didn't suit Durbin and the last three years of his life were spent as chaplain at the Motherhouse and Academy of the Sisters of the Third Order of St. Francis at Shelbyville.

Although somewhat diminutive in physical stature, Father Durbin was a giant in death.

Newspapers in Louisville and throughout the Southeast—together with Catholic publications throughout the nation—eulogized Durbin's death on March 22, 1887, at the convent of Franciscan Sisters in Shelbyville.

> (Editors note—Material used in this column was made available for publication by Brother Leo Willet, a native of Fancy Farm who moved with his family to St. Louis, MO, at an early age. Brother Willet spent 40 years as teacher and counselor at Chaminade College Prep School in St. Louis. He is a noted historian and researcher who presently is preparing a book on Catholicism in this area.)

Until now, Father Abell had been visiting Nashville as a mission, and then Father Durbin took charge. After about a year, he was assisted by Father Brown who made Ross Landing (now Chattanooga) his headquarters, just previous to the arrival of Bishop Miles in Nashville.

In 1837 Father Durbin addressed a letter to Bishop Guy Ignatius Chabrat SS, Coadjutor of the diocese at Bardstown, bearing the date of November 4, 1837, in which was the following passage:

> I am glad to hear of the nomination of Right Reverend R. P. (Richard Pius) Miles to the new See of Nashville, but I cannot consider myself released from that mission until I see him installed. I have promised to give two hundred dollars to help him fix himself up there. I hope you will urge others, both the priest and the people of the different congregations, to assist him liberally. (*The Centenary of Catholicity in Kentucky*)

To prepare for the coming of the Bishop, Father Durbin arrived in Nashville in the summer of 1837, took up a collection and had the church repaired and readied for services once again. Bishop Miles was consecrated September 16, 1838, in St. Joseph's Cathedral, Bardstown, and Father Durbin was one of the two priests present when he was installed in the Nashville church October 14th.

After guiding Bishop Miles on a 500-mile tour of the eastern portion of the state, Father Durbin returned to his post in Morganfield, Kentucky. His work in Tennessee was finished, except for an occasional urgent sick call, but he was to carry on his tremendous frontier missionary apostolate until death (*Historical Tribute to St. Thomas Seminary*, St. Louis, 1906).

In *Kentucky Pioneer and Descendants* is a section entitled *Caldwell County Marriages*. In this section is listed a marriage between William Kelly and Mildred A. Gracey, performed by E. J. Durbin, RCP. Undoubtedly, this is only one of probably hundreds of marriages he performed.

From a historical sketch entitled "St. Claire's Golden Jubilee, Altamont, Illinois 1925" sent to W. Jesse Durbin by Mrs. Louis P. (Leona Ann Logue) Schneiter of Taylorville, Illinois,

> Writing of St. Claire's Parish, that is including the mission place: The first priest to read Holy Mass in the parish was Reverend Father E. J. Durbin of Kentucky, in the year 1839. It has been related to me by Joseph Durbin, an early settler who met and conversed with Father Durbin, that the priest visited his scattered flock twice a year. He generally rode a white horse.

Mrs. Schneiter also sent Mr. Durbin a copy of an article from the International Encyclopedia. After a sketch of John Price Durbin, a Methodist minister, language college Professor, etc., 1800-1876, it states,

> His contemporary in Kentucky was Father Elisha Durbin, son of Blind John J. Durbin. Father Durbin was the first priest to say mass in St. Clair church at Altamont.

In 1845 and 1846, Father Durbin took on an assistant, Reverend James Quinn, who was ordained in 1844.

It is told that in 1850, Jack Roberts of Nelson County, Kentucky bequeathed to Father Durbin two "colored" slaves by the names of Charles and Jane Roberts. Father Durbin immediately sent them to Fancy Farm to serve the priests at St. Jerome parish there. They tended gardens and performed miscellaneous other tasks. In all, they bore five children, all Catholics. They later moved to St. Francis de Sales parish in Paducah. It was not until after the Civil War, fought from 1861 to 1865, that slavery was abolished in the United States. In 1850 Father Durbin had given these two slaves their freedom.

> In a book entitled *Sunfish/Edmonson County/Kentucky: Oasis of Catholicism* compiled by James H. Simon who was born and raised in Sunfish, are these words:

> In the death records of St. Vincent in Morganfield, Union County, Kentucky, written and kept by Father Elisha Durbin, are these notations:

>> Henrietta, servant of Rev. E.J. Durbin, 1842

>> Nace, servant of Rev. E.J. Durbin, 1852

>> Betty, wife of Nace, servant of Rev. E.J. Durbin, 1853

>> Basil, servant of Rev. E.J. Durbin, 1855

> This indicates to me that Father Durbin owned slaves, but perhaps that is not what it meant.

These "servants" more likely were volunteers or, similar to the Roberts family mentioned above, they were assigned by parishoners to work in the parish.

Mr. and Mrs. Ernest F. Schuchert of Chester, Randolph County, Illinois, provided W. Jesse Durbin with this account:

> Reverend Elisha Durbin, born in Madison County, Kentucky in 1800, died in 1887. First resident priest at Shawneetown, Illinois in 1839. Had sole charge of Illinois as far north as Vandalia. Served 37 years in Southern Illinois.

During the American Civil War, Father Durbin expanded his duties by caring for the religious needs of the soldiers from both sides of the conflict.

Volume II, *The Appleton Cyclopaedia of American Biography*, says that Father Durbin estimated that over a period of sixty-two years (actually 65 years) he has traveled over 500,000 miles. Also to his credit are the many churches he erected. In 1873 he was relieved of his pastoral duties in Union County, but insisted on being allotted active work, and was given charge of the Roman Catholics living along the Elizabethtown and Paducah railroad.

In the 1800's the railroad business was booming in many parts of the country and Western Kentucky was no exception. Towns emerged from sparsely populated fields and pastures along the lines. The railroad continued that tradition of giving birth to small towns when it came to the Hopkins County area and helped bestow municipal life upon the area known as White Plains. The area that became White Plains had been known for many years as "Little Prairie." For nearly 70 years the Cherokee Indians of Tennessee would burn the ground of Little Prairie to provide a large grazing area for buffalo and deer. The Cherokee would repeatedly come into the area, setting up camps to hunt and fish, but left the area in 1836 for good, to migrate west of the Mississippi into the Indian Territory. Later, when the railroad system passed through the area, White Plains was a community in Christian County. Because "Little Prairie," located in Hopkins County, was on the Elizabethtown and Paducah railroad line, it was the logical place for supplies bound for White Plains to be shipped. So, "Little Prairie" became known as White Plains Station and eventually New White Plains.

Also affected by the railroad, the southwesternmost point in Jefferson County, "Valley" has long existed in splendid isolation, only half-jokingly viewed by its residents and outsiders alike as having as much in common with neighboring Bullitt, Meade and Hardin counties as with Louisville. Because of its isolation and limited space for homes and farms, Valley was only sparsely populated during its first century or more of existence. A small railroad station—one of many along the tracks of the old Elizabethtown & Paducah Railroad—gave the settlement its name and provided a handy way for residents to ride in to the city and back. While the Elizabethtown & Paducah railroad was crossing Muhlenberg County east to west in the 1870s, a second railroad, the Louisville & Nashville, was traversing the county, north to south. Samuel Thomas III (1811–1874), son of Samuel Jr. and Mary (Howard) moved to Kentucky and became Director and First President of the Elizabethtown and Paducah Railroad. He ammassed a large fortune and much of his property was in Louisville, Kentucky. He married Zorayda Young.

Father Durbin remained in this capacity, ministering to the people living by the railroad, until 1883 when he was persuaded to spend the remainder of his life in St. Joseph's Seminary in Bardstown. In 1885 he petitioned his bishop to be restored to active duty, and was again assigned to pastoral work.

This, then, was the life that the zealous Father Durbin endured for over sixty years. Much of the information herein was gleaned from a book by the Honorable Benjamin J. Webb, whose credentials should be explored here.

Chapter 7

▼

The Tangled Webb

Precious little has been written about the life of Father Elisha John Durbin. However, Benjamin Joseph Webb has written excerpts on the lives of the most important Catholic figures to play roles in the growth and maintenance of Catholicism in the early days of Kentucky. Included in these excerpts is Honorable Webb's high praise of Father Durbin.

Honorable Benjamin Joseph Webb

Benjamin Joseph Webb was an editor and historian. He was born at Bardstown, Kentucky February 25, 1814, and died at Louisville, Kentucky August 2, 1897. His father, Nehemiah Webb, was a convert to Catholicism and he was one of the pioneers of Kentucky in 1774. Nehemiah was a millwright and is credited with erecting and operating the first cotton gin and the first oil press in the State (*The Centenary of Catholicity in Kentucky*). Benjamin was educated at St. Joseph's College, Bardstown, which he left at an early age to learn the printer's trade. He was foreman of the office of the *Journal*, a newspaper in Louisville, when, in 1836, the Rev. Dr. Reynolds (later Bishop of Charleston, South Carolina), who had been one of his teachers at St. Joseph's, persuaded him to undertake the publication at Bardstown of the *Catholic Advocate*. This paper, with the assistance of Bishops Spalding, David, and Flaget, he successfully conducted; he removed its office to Louisville in 1841, and in 1847 retired from its management. He continued, however, to defend Catholic interests, notably in connection with George D. Prentice, editor of the Louisville *Courier-Journal* in 1855, in a series of letters on the intolerance of Knownothingism, which had disgraced the city by the atrocities of "Bloody Monday." Knownothingism, along with another notorious group, will be covered in the next chapter.

Honorable Webb's letters were printed subsequently in book form with the title, *Letters of a Kentucky Catholic*. On May 1, 1858, at the insistence of Bishop Spalding and in connection with other members of the Particular Council of the St. Vincent de Paul Society of Louisville, he issued the *Catholic Guardian*, which the Civil War troubles ended in July 1862. He was also a contributor to the *Catholic Advocate* on its revival in 1869.

His long association with Catholic interests in Kentucky prompted him to compile *The Centenary of Catholicity in Kentucky* (Louisville, 1884), a volume invaluable in its records of the men and times of the pioneer era. He served as a member of the state senate from Louisville during the years 1867-1875, and in 1868 wrote, at the request of the Legislature, *Memoirs of Gov. Lazarus W. Powell and Gov. John L. Helm* (published by the State). During his life he was justly regarded as the foremost Catholic layman of Kentucky.

The preceding narrative on Benjamin Webb is paraphrased from *History of the Ohio Falls Cities* (Cleveland, 1882); *The Record and Catholic Advocate* (Louisville), contemporary files. It was compiled by Thomas F. Meehan and transcribed by Thomas M. Barrett, dedicated to the memory of Benjamin Joseph Webb. It can be found in the *Catholic Encyclopedia*, copyright © 1913 by the Encyclopedia Press, Inc. (Electronic version copyright © 1997 by New Advent, Inc.)

In his book, the Honorable Benjamin J. Webb narrates the life of Father Durbin from a historical perspective. This chapter is Webb's story, and the superscript numbers show which page(s) of his book contain the information.

Elisha J. Durbin was born in Madison County, Kentucky, about sixteen miles from Boonesboro, on the first day of February 1800. His parents were John J. Durbin and Patience Logsdon. The interest that is exhibited in my labors, at the cost of time and pains has been taken by...Reverend E. J. Durbin....PAGE 10, "ACKNOWLEDGMENTS"

The diocesan seminary of St. Thomas was established in 1811, under the direction of Reverend John B. David, and from that date to the year 1824, quite a number of priests were ordained from the ranks of its students. Among them it is only necessary here to mention the following, Reverends Chabrat, Schaeffer, Ganihl, Derigaud, Deparcq, Horstman, Abell, Elder, William Byrne, Reynolds, McMahon, Robert Byrne and Elisha J. Durbin.^{PAGE 27}

Following are remembrances of Rev. J. M. Higgins, St. Vincent, Union County, as sent to Mother Agnes.

> Reverend Elisha J. Durbin and His Missionary Labors In the Owensboro Diocese
>
> Introduction
>
> The first Catholics to come to the Owensboro Diocese arrived about 1805. These moved west from Washington and Marion, and settled in Hardinsburgh, Hardin and Union Counties. The spiritual wants of these scattered few were at first attended to by Father Nerinckx and later by Father Robert A. Abell.
>
> From *Catholicity in Kentucky*, by Ben Webb, we read, "Union County was organized In 1811. It was several years before Catholics of considerable numbers were led to its fertile fields in selection of their future homes. Previous to the year 1818, it is likely there were not a dozen Catholic families settled in the county."
>
> However, September 13, 1818, the Reverend Abell, a young priest, was given charge of this portion of the Lord's Vineyard, now known as the Owensboro Diocese.
>
> By pre-arrangement, Ben Webb tells us, the young Abell and the retiring pastor set out together for a visitation of the widely scattered people of this district. Although this was Father Abell's first missionary trip, Father Nerinckx Insisted on his performing all the pastoral duties, he himself occupying the humble position of 'altar boy' as he himself playfully called it.
>
> Their first objective point was Saint Ignatius, Hardin County. From this Point they went to Elizabethtown. Their next stop was at Hardinsburg where Father Nerinckx had built the

church, Saint Anthony in 1812-1816. This was called the 'fair weather church,' as it was roofless for several years.

Extending their missionary tour, they reached Morganfield in Union County, where Father Abell preached a lengthy discourse in the Court House. He was the hero of the hour, and as a result of the labors of the joint missionaries, 105 acres were donated for the erection of a Catholic school.

After a three weeks stay in Union County, the missionaries proceeded beyond the diocese to Saint Theresa, Flint Island, where Father Abell preached and they were presented with 300 acres of land for church and school.

Father Abell fixed his home at Saint Anthony, Hardinsburg, the central point of his mission, satisfied that his congregations would only gain by the change of pastors, Father Nerinckx entrusted to the energetic Father Abell all the missions situated in this new district and hurried back to his dear Loretto, where other work awaited him.

The appointment of Father Durbin as resident pastor at Sacred Heart in 1824 moved the center of operation from Hardinsburg to Union County, and was of tremendous importance to Catholics of that section.

Father Durbin lived for God as can be seen by all the spiritual advantages he gave his flock. On October 30, 1841, from the Editor of the Catholic Advocate, we may read the following about the Spiritual Retreats given in many of his missions. Reverend and dear Editor:

"The Catholic Congregations of Union, Daviess, Hardinsburg, and Flint Island, have just enjoyed the benefits of a Spiritual Retreat. This holy and salutary religious exercise was opened at the Sacred Heart, Union County. Reverend Evremond, S. J. was the retreat master at each place. Reverend E. J. Durbin gave one or two discourses each day on the sacraments of Penance and the Eucharist. The ardent zeal, the fervent piety of these two Reverend Gentlemen are too well known to need the eulogy of my feeble pen."

The retreats began September 5 and ended at Saint Theresa, Flint Island on October 15.

Communicants in Union County	232
Communicants in Davies County	230
Communicants in Hardinsburg	100
Communicants at Flint Island	230
Communicants at two stations in Davies	59

On Tuesday September 28, 1841, the new and elegant little church of Hardinsburg was blessed by Bishop Flaget, assisted by his V. G., Very Reverend I. A. Reynolds and Reverend Messrs. Evremond, S. J., Rogers, Wathen, Durbin, and Adams. Reverend Mr. Reynolds preached the dedication sermon. The weather was bad, and the audience, in consequence, rather small.

Again we read in the Advocate:

On October 1, 1840, the Bishop preached to a large congregation in the Court House of Morganfield; and on the next day he made the visitation at the Church of Saint Ambrose, consisting of 15 families. This church is a neat brick structure, amply large for those who at present attend it. Adjoining the church is a farm of 200 acres deeded to the Bishop in trust for the congregation. Besides the two congregations above named the Reverend Mr. Durbin attends several stations lying in this and the adjoining counties.

The Reverend W. E. Clarke and Coomes accompanied the Bishop to Henderson on October 28, 1840, where he preached in the Court House to a large, attentive audience. There are not more than a half dozen Catholics in this place. From Henderson the Bishop proceeded to the Sacred Heart, now a parish of 150 families, where he confirmed 236. Twenty of these were converts. The Bishop exhorted the people to build a new Church, as the chapel is much too small for the congregation.

On October 24, 1849, the Bishop visited the congregation of Saint Raphael on Panther Creek where he confirmed 49. This is a new settlement of 32 families. There is a log chapel in the midst of the woods, situated on a farm of 200 acres of good land belonging to the Church.

Catholic Advocate, October 25, 1849

Dear Editor:

On September 28th the Bishop Coadjutor of Louisville reached Owensborough, accompanied by the Reverend D. A. Deparcq. On the following day the retreat was opened at the church of Saint Stephen, a neat brick edifice in the lower part of the town.

The Reverend W. S. Coomes, pastor of the congregation was assisted by the Reverend Messrs. Deparcq and Coghlan, the Reverend W. E. Clarke having gone on in advance to the next congregation on Panther Creek to instruct the children for Confirmation. The attendance at Saint Stephen was good, and the Retreat closed on Sunday the twenty-third with a general Communion and the Episcopal Visitation. The Bishop preached four times during the continuance of the exercises, and on Sunday administered confirmation to 69. There were 105 communicants. The Bishop made suitable arrangements for the support of the pastor.

This little congregation is composed of about 35 families, many of whom live a distance from the church. A lot adjoining the church had been purchased for the Sisters of Charity of Nazareth; and a female Academy will be opened by them in a hired house early in next November. Many protestants attended the instructions and seemed well disposed. Altogether the prospects of the congregation are promising.

It was Father Durbin who first said Mass at Saint Stephens.

Bishop Flaget confirmed here in 1841.

In the course of time the flock, small on his arrival at Sacred Heart, and which had grown rapidly up to the building of the church in 1828, had so far increased in numbers, as to need a more spacious edifice than that which had succeeded the log hut chapel.

At the advice of his Bishop a new church of stately form and adequate dimensions was erected through the incessant labors of Father Durbin. The new church was made sacred by having its first Mass on Christmas Day, the birthday of Christ the King, in 1855.

On June 1856 there was a great gathering to witness the dedication of this new Sacred Heart Church at Saint Vincent by Right Reverend Martin John Spalding, assisted by the pastor, Father Durbin, and by Fathers Bouchet and Oberhulsman, Bishop Spalding delivered an eloquent sermon. (Author's Note: This gathering actually took place on June 20, 1855.)

In his *Story of the Catholic Church of Paducah* Mr. J.T. Donovan writes: "Since the establishment of Catholicity in Western Kentucky is so intimately associated with the memory of Father Elisha J. Durbin, no history of the Church in Paducah can be complete without extended mention of that saintly missionary. Through scorching sun and chilly snows, over dusty and muddy roads, he rode with saddle-bags across his horse over all that region in Kentucky west of Jefferson County visiting the few scattered and isolated Catholic families and individuals, offering up the Holy Sacrifice of the Mass and administering the Sacraments in farm houses, country stores and barns, gradually forming congregations, building schools and churches, securing priests to serve and act as assistants in his missionary work in widely separated settlements.

Before the Church was built at Paducah, services were held at the home of John Greif. There also, the missionaries and the resident pastors made their homes until the first rectory was erected. The building, still standing, is the home of the Woman's Club of Paducah. The baptismal register of Saint Francis de Sales shows that Father Durbin continued his missionary work in the vicinity of Paducah, and often visited there to administer the Sacraments, even after a residential pastor had been appointed. He performed these ministrations since the first pastors were assistant missionaries and at times absent caring for the needs of Catholics in adjacent territory; moreover, as Father Durbin had served the Catholics of

Paducah for years, and had become greatly loved, many of them wished that he still serve them as favorable occasions arose.

Father Durbin had great veneration for Saint Francis de Sales. The original members of the congregation detected traits of similarity between the saintly prelate and their beloved missionary.

The colored members of the congregation of Paducah are nearly all descendants of two slaves, man and wife, bequeathed to Father Durbin by Jack Roberts of Nelson County, Kentucky about 1850. They were set free by Father Durbin. He sent them to Fancy Farm to serve the priests of Saint Jerome parish. In 1862 they moved to Paducah with their five children.

Father Durbin like Father Nerinckx goes down in History as a church builder.

St. Agnes, Uniontown, makes the fifth link of churches under his pastorate. Though used from 1860, it was finished several years later under the direction of Rev. J. M. Martin, D. D., assistant of Father Durbin at the Sacred Heart.

It is said that on the day of laying the corner stone of Saint Agnes, the weather was so disagreeable, Father Durbin repaired to the Baptist church at the invitation of some if its members, and there delivered the sermon of the day.

The lot upon which the church stands was donated by Wm. David, a non-Catholic.

The church of Saint Anne, Morganfield, belongs properly to a later date. The site upon which the church of Saint Anne stands was a gift from Hon. I. A. Spalding, Sr., whose house had been a church station of the town. All were anxious to know the name of the new church. The Bishop settled the matter thus: Tiding along with good old Father Durbin the Bishop asked, "What is the Christian name of Mrs. Spalding?" Father Durbin answered, "Why, Aunt Nancy." "Anne then is the name of the church," said the Bishop.

As Father Durbin's missionary field was growing to such an extent, Reverend Michael Bouchet was made his assistant for Henderson in 1853. This field had been attended by Father Durbin since 1824.

The first move for a church in Henderson was in 1858 under the direction of Reverend William Burke, but Father Dunn, assistant of Father Durbin, became its first resident pastor. The church was called Saint Louis.

1872—Golden Jubilee of Father Durbin

At the Golden Jubilee of Father Durbin, two thousand people were present. But where was the Jubilee? Let the speaker of the day, Honorable T. A. Spalding, Sr., tell you. He says, 'Other men can entertain their friends in parlors and diningrooms, but Father Durbin's friends can be entertained only in the boundless forest, at the bounteous banquet board of an old Kentucky Barbecue.' The elegant feast and the immense crowd that partook of it were most touching and merited compliment to Father Durbin.

After Mr. Spalding, the Venerable Robert Abell, himself a priest for fifty-four years spoke of the outstanding accomplishments of Father Durbin's long and truly wonderful clerical life.

In view of his remarkable record it is not strange that his friends should have given him such an entertainment on his fiftieth anniversary as a priest, nor that two thousand people should attend this festival.

At the great banquet Father Durbin told an amusing story of his early priestly life.

"Shortly after I was ordained," he said, "I was in Bardstown one day and met old General Joe Lewis, and he said in his peculiar squeaking voice, 'Durbin, when you are going to preach, I would like to hear you."

I told him I didn't suppose he would hear much of a sermon, if he should hear me.

"No," said he, "and if I did, it would surprise me very much."

"On the day I was to preach my first sermon, I sent the general word that if he desired to hear what I would be able to say, he should attend church at late Mass that day."

"I had my notes prepared and got along pretty smoothly for fifteen minutes, but I got the notes mixed somehow, which confused me very much, and the rest of my sermon was not very interesting."

"A day or two afterwards I heard the General telling some of his friends about it. He said, 'It started off first rate, and kept right ahead for awhile, but he ran his canoe in the bushes and never did get it out again.'"

The last commencement attended by Father Durbin at his dear home, St. Vincent, was in 1881. His address on this occasion was: "Home, Heaven is our True Home." However, after the consecration of Dr. Rademacker in Tennessee (1883) he visited Union County.

A letter written by Father Durbin to Mr. Johnson, a convert of Rev. James Pike at Beech Grove in 1885, begins: "I saw Father Pike at St. Vincent last week who told me he had taken you into the Church, etc."

To the Editor of the Catholic Review:

Father Abell visited Nashville, but I don't know what years, nor how often. Probably under his administration a church was built. If I mistake not, no priest was stationed in Nashville before Bishop Miles, except one, E.J. Durbin.

Bearing date, Nov. 4, 1837, is shown in the Catholic Advocate a letter of Father Durbin to the Coadjutor Bishop of the Diocese: "I am glad to hear of the nomination of Right Rev. R. R. Miles to the new See of Nashville. But I cannot feel myself released from that mission until I see him installed. I have promised to give $200 to help him fix himself up there. I hope you will urge others, both the priests and the people of the different congregations to assist him liberally.

REMINISCENCES

Everybody loved Father Durbin. Altho' dead now many years the young generation of his day still refer to him as "Good Old Father Durbin," and love to relate incidents and circumstances that still linger among the happy memories of bygone years and feelings.

"Oh, I remember when he said Mass in our house, which was called a church station. I can see him coming on horseback, wearing a big gray shawl, his arms flopping up and down with the motion of his trotting horse."

Another tells of Father being at his house when the narrator was a little chap four or five years old, and that he followed a penitent upstairs to peep in to see what was going on. Father beckoned him to come in. He ran away instead.

Mrs. Hammerstein, his housekeeper says he came home many a time with his coat and hat frozen to him. After riding all night, he would rush to the confessional, his place of rest. It was Father Durbin's custom to have the rosary recited before Mass. He also insisted on family prayer morning and evening, a custom which prevails in many Catholic homes.

When our Father Durbin was seen coming home on his old white 'nag,' all the girls at St. Vincent would run out to meet him.

Volumes could be filled with reminiscences of the kindheartedness and generosity of the good Father. In a true, helpful, pioneer spirit, he added offices to his distinctive one of pastor. As there was not a post-office in his vicinity, Father Durbin was mail-carrier. On Saturdays he brought from the nearest town, Morganfield, the mail for the Sisters, their pupils, and the various households near by. The mail bag was carried to the sacristy of the chapel where it was emptied on the floor, the letters then being claimed by their rightful owners. This primitive method of distribution may seem questionable, but under the supervision of Father Durbin, who knew his flock so well, it was evidently safe.

Mrs. Logan, wife of General Logan, writes: "Girls were sent to St. Vincent under the care of Father Durbin. In the wide territory of his missionary labors, this 'Patriotic priest' won many devoted friends among non-Catholics as well as Catholics who gladly entrusted their children to his fatherly care. After the custom of those stage-coach days, many a time at the beginning of school sessions, there might be seen a merry caravan, a flock of S.V.A. pupils wending their way to the Academy, shepherded by Father Durbin. Parents far and near esteemed convent training. The 'convent bred' girl was looked upon as an attraction."

In the Indiana Centennial celebration of 1916, the Kentucky Academy of Union County was accorded representation because of its share in the education of Indiana girls. In the pageant parade were seven girls, daughters and granddaughters of former pupils who had attended S.V.A. in Father Durbin's pastorate, garbed in the uniform purple dresses, white collars, cuffs, and belts—a charming group against a background showing a picture of the Old Academy. At the opposite end of the float, the modern S. V. A. girls were grouped against a similar background, picturing the later buildings of this famous school. In the center between the old and the new, by a cross inscribed "To the Memory of Father Durbin," Father Oberhulsman, as no one else could, impersonated the beloved priest, whose coming meant so much to generations dead and gone.

But for Father Durbin there was no time for idleness on earth. He besought his bishop to be permitted to serve once in active duty. Not knowing how to refuse the glowing fervor of the aged priest the Bishop assigned the chaplaincy of Sts. Mary and Elizabeth Hospital, in the city, and leaving there, we see him later on, where he wrought his last days' work in his Master's vineyard, chaplain at Shelbyville, to the Convent of the Franciscan nuns. A chaplain within the limits of that great territory he once had served alone.

Cronology of Rev. Elisha J. Durbin

1800—Born near Boonesboro, Madison County, Kentucky.
1816—Entered the Seminary at Bardstown.
1821—Master of ceremonies at St. Rose of consecration Bishop Fenwick.
1822—Ordained at Bardstown by Bishop David.
1822—Made assistant at Cathedral. Taught at St. Joseph' College.
1824—Pastor of Western Kentucky, center at Sacred Heart.
1828—Retreats and confirmations of this imense parish by Father Durbin and Bishop Flaget.
1828—Sacred Heart, Union County dedicated by Bishop Flaget.
1829—His first assistant for St. Ambrose—Rev. R. E. Clarke.
1830—Built St. Ambrose
1836—Built St. Jerome, Fancy Farm, McCracken County. Said Mass at St. John's before a church was built.
1840—Visitation of Bishop Flaget.
1841—Retreats of the diocese by Fathers Durbin and Evermond, S.J.
1841—Said Mass at St. Stephens, Owensboro.
1841—Dedication of church at Hardinsburg.
1848—Built St. Francis de Sales, Paducah.
1849—Retreat at St. Stephens, Owensboro.
1855—First Mass at new Sacred Heart Church, St. Vincent, Ky.
1856—Dedication of Sacred Heart Church by Bishop Flaget.
1858—St Jerome, Fancy Farm, dedicated.
1858—St. Louis, Henderson, built.
1860—Cornerstone of St. Agnes, Uniontown.
1862—St. Louis, Henderson, dedicated.
1869—St. John, McCracken. Note by Father Durbin.
1872—Golden Jubilee in the woods at Morganfield.
1878—St. Anne, Morganfield, dedicated.
1880—Cornerstone of St. Benedict, Beech Grove.
1881—Came from Princeton to Morganfield to give them Mass.
1881—Attended his last commencement at S.V.A.
1883—Consecration of Bishop Miles in Tenn.
1883—Attended consecration of Dr. Rademacker, Tenn.
1884—Jubilee Missions throughout diocese.
1885—His last visit to S. V. A. Found in Father J. Pike's scrapbook.
1887—Death at Shelbyville.
1887—Burial in St. Louis Cemetery.

FATHER DURBIN'S SIXTY-FOURTH ANNIVERSARY

"I have now this day been sixty-four years a Priest,__saying Mass every day all that time, when ever it was convenient for me to do so, and sometimes when it wasn't convenient." These simple awe-inspiring words fell from the lips of the venerable Father Durbin, as he stood on the altar steps at the Seminary on Tuesday last, addressing the students. The discourse as a whole struck all who heard it, both priests and seminarians, as singularly happy:—a Very gem of eloquence in its clear flow of simple words giving utterance to deep truths, in their own natural paths.

The students accomplished well their part in the celebration, by singing a beautiful Mass. After breakfast they surrounded the good Father for a recreation day; and after some pleasant repartee between the young clerics and the aged priest, he said to their great joy: "Well, I reckon you may have it, if it will do you any good." Later in the day, he entertained them with stories of his early experience on the mission; telling them, among other things, that he was born in the diocese of Baltimore, though he had never been out of Kentucky:___ a conundrum. which some of our readers can 'give up,' without any imputation on their cleverness.

DEATH OF FATHER DURBIN March 22, 1887 (From an old Scrap Book at Mt. St. Joseph)

Rev. Elisha J. Durbin, a pioneer Priest of Kentucky, and the second oldest priest in the United States, died on Tuesday, March 22nd, in Shelbyville, at the age of 87 years.

The octogenarian Father came in with the century. He was born at Richmond, Madison county, Ky., on February 1st 1800, ordained Priest at Bardstown, September 21st, 1822, and for 65 years has laboured as such in this diocese. He was one of the pioneer Priests of Kentucky who at the cost of much hardship and privation cleared the ground and planted the mustard seed which has grown to be the wide spreading tree of today. In 1824 he was sent to Morganfield, in Union county, then embracing a circuit of 150 miles. About the time he reached his seventieth year he often became very weak from heart disease. Several times he fell from his horse while making his rounds. Repeatedly had the Bishop invited him in view of his great age, to retire from the constant labour of the pastorate, before he could bring himself to give up his beloved parish. He then took charge of a church at Princeton, Ky., and after a few years went to Bardstown. He next came to this city and was for a while chaplain of the Sts. Mary and Elizabeth Hospital.

About three years ago he went to Shelbyville, and ministered to the Sisters until his death of old age, on Tuesday, 22nd.

RE—REV. E.J. DURBIN

Dear Mother Agnes:

This should have been written long since, but of late I have been so busy with work that had to be taken care of that I simply could not get to it. Mother, this is about all I can find here of the life of father Durbin. We have all his baptismal records and many of the death records, no marriage records. If you would have a chance to come down sometime I would be happy to show you over these record. I have had a copy of them all made and I will bring it with me some of these days when I am coming up but that is not like seeing the record book as written out in his own hand. I am sure you know the Sister who did this work. She is a sister of father Will Pike late of Bardstown. You may keep this copy. I had it taken from the original here in the library. I hope it will prove of some help to you. If there has been such a life of the venerable old pastor as you referred to in your letter, I know nothing of it.

With kindest personal regards,

(signed) John M. Higgins

NOTE—The above letter explains the enclosed M. S. Life of the Rev. E. J. Durbin sent by Rev. J. M. Higgins, St. Vincent, Union County, to Mother Agnes in response to her request for the life-sketch of the Patriarch of the Church in the Diocese of Owensboro. The author of the M. S. is Sister Agnes Marie Pike of the Sisters of Charity of Nazareth.

May 8, 1940

Mother M. Agnes

Analist of M. S. J."

Of some interest here, W. Jesse Durbin wrote to a cousin of his, Sister Mary Loretta, an Ursuline nun. Her birth name is Matilda May "Mayo" Durbin.

Morrisonville, Illinois 62546

Nov. 5, 1968.

Sister Loretta Durbin,

Maple Mount, Kentucky 42356.

Dear Sister and Friend,

At last I have gotten around to the pleasure of answering your appreciated interchange of June 17, 1968. Pardon my seeming lack of interest, it seems I get slower and more dilatory with my writing as the years ago by. But come the 18th of this month I will be 89 so I reckon one naturally slows down with age. And I have several correspondents on my mailing list, as do most people who write genealogy.

A distant relative, Ted Durbin, made a run to Kentucky recently and visited among others in Edmondson County one Sam Durbin of Sunfish and made notes of his family line. He is grandson of John Durbin brother of Joseph Durbin your grandfather. As I get from him, John Durbin, brother of Father Elisha Durbin and son of Blind John D. Durbin, married Rebecca Logsdon. She was a daughter of William Logsdon, son of Edward and Polly (Brown) Logsdon. John and Rebecca Logsdon's son, Dr. John Durbin, born in 1820, and wife had the following children:

Joseph, John, George A. (Sam's father, Elijah and Christopher Durbin).

George A. Durbin's children were:

George, John, Joseph, Sam, Tom, Becky, Marie, Hannah, Melinda, Margaret and twins Nancy and Lucy Durbin. George A. married Lucy Whobre. Sam married Mary Hayes.

But it seems most of the Durbins have migrated from Grayson and Edmondson counties.

I would like to send an offering to Rev. J. Higgins and would if I had the means to do so. But being on old age assistance I cannot always meet the church dues, Parish and Diocesan, as we are only allowed scant enough to get by on. His name recalls to mind that I went to catechism instructions to a Father Higgins, or leastwise to church when he was a priest at St. Mary's parish at Taylorville, Illinois. Maybe some time later I may find means to comply with your wish about the offering for the back spiritual notes of Father Higgins.'

It seems you had a brother living when you wrote. I have a sister living. She resides at Tucumcari, New Mexico. Her sister daughter is with her at present to help her mother and doing Parish religion instructions or teaching and also helping care for aged needy women. My sister will be 87 in Dec. and her health is not the best has high blood pressure but manages to attend 6:00 mass daily when weather or street conditions are not to bad.

I guess there is little more to mention. Hope you are as well as usual or better. Your arthritis no worse. Arthritis is a crippling disease. The sister of the new neighbor recently moved here has arthritis in her back and uses two canes to get about.

Her brother also limps from an injury he received. I don't think she ever married but he was but is widowed I think. I was acquainted with them at Palmer, Ill. some years ago. At that time his sister was keeping his two daughters for him all marrying later.

Well may God bless and keep you in his holy care.

Sincerely yours W. J. Durbin"

This is what Sister Loretta Durbin says about herself, and this is followed by her obituary.

"Sister Loretta Durbin statistics:

Baptismal name: Matilda (or Mayo?)
Born Jan. 20, 1895, Sunfish, Ky.
Entered Novitiate: Dec. 8, 1915

Invested (received habit): Mar. 25, 1916
Made First Vows: Aug. 5, 1918
Died: July 9, 1973
Father: William Henry Durbin
Mother: Elizabeth Yates
Brother: James Elvie Durbin, Sacramento, Ky.
Other contacts: Elvie Durbin & Mrs. Ida Lohman, Rumsey, Ky.

"Missions:

Mt. St. Joseph	1915-1916
Fairfield, Ky.	1916-1917
Stanley, Ky.	1917-1918
St. Charles, Lebanon, Ky.	1918-1920
Dixon, Neb.	1920-1921
Wynot, Neb.	1921-1922
Snyder, Neb.	1922-1924
Nebraska City, Neb.	1925-1930
Mt. St. Joseph	1930-1932
Howardstown, Ky.	1932-1933
Holy Cross, Ky.	1933-1934
Mt. St. Joseph	1934-1939
Rome, Ky.	1939-1940
St. Denis, Louisville, Ky.	1940-1941
Mt. St. Joseph	1941-1943
Knottsville, Ky.	1943-1944
Leitchfield, Ky.	1944-1945
Rome, Ky.	1945-1946
Cloverport, Ky.	1946-1947
St. Joseph, Raywick, Ky.	1947-1949
Wilhelmina, Missouri	1949-1950
Knottsville, Ky.	1950-1953
Raywick, Ky. St. Francis	1953-1954
Mt. St. Joseph	1954-1955
Leitchfield, Ky.	1955-1956
Mt. St. Joseph	1957-(died July 9, 1973)

"1965—A Brief Autobiography or, What My Friends are Saying About the Durbin Gal of Rumsey, Kentucky.

"Well, I do declare, they say the Durbin gal is going be an Ursuline Sister. Where did the idea come from? No one but the dear Lord would think of such a thing. Talk about Tom-boy girls, she was a first class one. She had two small brothers with whom she played and naturally she took up their ways, rough-and-tumble at times. Another thing that surprises the neighbors was her lack of dignity. What is the difference? Gold must be refined and so must we. God did his own refining and before anyone could detect the change, she was ready to become the Bride of Christ. Playing at hide-and-seek with those brothers, Sister had as a girl jumped out of the barn loft or from the highest cliffs. She could swing on a grapevine or from the types of birches Robert Frost loved so well. "Dignity" she thought, "was for the Pope or priest." Some of her neighbors mused, "can any good come from Rumsey"? The answer is "Come and see."

The first sorrow that came into her life was at the age of three. This tiny little girl ran away from home rather than take the spanking that was due. On his return Papa Durbin found his family in a state of excitement; all looking for the lost child but she was nowhere to be found. Finally someone thought perhaps she had gone to her grandmother's which was three miles away. Yes, she was on her way and as she passed the first neighbor's house, the neighbors tried to get her to come in, but, Durbin-like she would not be detained. On she tripped and soon Papa Durbin was on her trail. He caught up with the runaway after she had passed three homes and he was very happy to find his darling child. He picked her up, kissed her fondly, and carried her on his shoulders to the very door step. All were happy at the return of the 'little prodigal,' and a kind and loving sister, Florence, served the refreshments that restored her to health and happiness again. No one had to sing "Tuck Me To Sleep In My Old Kentucky Home" nor did this little one need to be rocked to sleep on that particular night. My dear father lived to be ninty-three years old and this is beyond my comprehension.

He worked hard all the years of his life and was never known to have a vacation. I like to recall the time I was holding a log for Jake and Elvie and either the log or I slipped and my thumb was cut off. My good Father had to ride horse-back three miles to take me to the Doctor.

With my hand all bandaged up I would now get out of some of the work, like the dish washing and the churning which I disliked so much. But, I am convinced that I will be not able to fool St. Peter at the Golden Gate unless I put my hand, the one with the missing thumb, behind me. My Guarding Angel will be there to prevent any fraud, however, and he will help me reach the beautiful…in heaven.

The next chapter of this autobiography will be added later. Country talk never stops. One says, talk about dignity. That Durbin Gal is far from it. Her call reminds me of the time that Christ called the poor Fishermen to follow Him. She is a poor fish to catch, not good enough for a Fri. meal.

The five young Durbins were not as dumb as they look. They heard that certain candy was good for colds. We all coughed. It worked. We got the candy.

Florence often asked me if some one asked me to deny Christ, what would I do? I thought I would manage it some way. I did not know that I would lead a martyr's life in my own home. My brothers thought I ought to be perfect in cooking and in keeping my temper. One said, 'I'll give her two weeks in the Convent.' March 25, 1966 will be my Golden Jubillee in the Convent. How about this, dear Brother.

All the Durbins turned out very well except the Durbin Gal. She has tried to climb the ladder of Love to Christ's Heart. She has the key that unlocks it, but has not reached the heights of Holiness. I knew all the time that she ought to stay at Rumsey, and live like the rest of us. In her teen age she attracted suiters but no one suiter suited her.

Amid Joys and Sorrows of life I heard a faint whisper of Christ, "Come and follow me. I will make you a flame of My Love. Say you will be mine." Lord I am not worthy to be your Bride. Do with me as you will. The Divine Call came when I was alone reading the Bible. After receiving this call to follow Christ, nothing more in this world could satisfy my heart.

To say goood-bye is hard. Some cried. Some said funny things. One said, "You will be married before me." Another said, "you will go to the Mount and get stuck up."

My Vow Day was August 5, 1918. On this day I became the Bride of Jesus. I can now call Him Bridegroom, Lover and Spouse. In Christ's palace there are servants to take care of things. The Queen must charm Him with her love. There is no sacrifice too great to follow Jesus. I hope when life is over that I will be ready to meet Him.

I am now awaiting my eternal Home-going. In my suffering I try to make up for the past. I want my last word to be said in love. "Oh Jesus, I love you and want the whole world to love you."

Author unknown.

Imprimatur.   Bisbop of Rumsey, Kentucky
(This was in fun.)

Obituary: SISTER MARY L. DURBIN

Sister Mary Loretta Durbin, 78, died Monday at Mount Saint Joseph after a long illness. She was born Jan. 20, 1895 in Sunfish, Ky. She was a member of the Mount Saint Joseph Ursuline Community for 57 years. She had served schools in Daviess and Marion Counties, Ky., and in Nebraska. She had been retired at Mount Saint Joseph since 1956.

Survivors include one brother, James Elvie Durbin, Sacramento, Ky. and several nieces and nephews.

Funeral services will be held at 10 a.m. Wednesday in the Chapel at the Mount Saint Joseph Academy with the Rev. Bernard Powers, pastor of Mount Saint Joseph Convent, officiating. Burial will be in Mount Saint Joseph Cemetery.

Friends may call after 1 p.m. today at Mount Saint Joseph. Delbert J. Glenn Funeral Home has charge of arrangements.

Sister Mary Loretta Durbin, besides being quite a character, is a grandniece of Father Elisha John Durbin. We now continue with B. J. Webb's history of Catholicity in Kentucky.

The Home of Rachel and William Coomes of Owensboro was a station and resting place for Fathers Nerinckx, Abell, Durbin and other priests in their visitations to that part.^{PAGE 38} In 1845 and 1846 Reverend James Quinn was the assistant to Reverend Elisha J. Durbin on the missions of southwestern Kentucky.^{PAGE 40} Reverend Edward Clark associated with Reverend Elisha J. Durbin in the mission of Union and adjoining counties.^{PAGE 55}

In 1791, a year before Kentucky was admitted into the confederation of states, there were settled within its borders no fewer than six distinct and large colonies of Catholics, five of which were in the single county of Nelson. These were known as Pottinger's Creek, Bardstown or Poplar Neck, Cartwright's Creek, Hardin's Creek, Rolling Fork Settlements (all in Nelson County) and Woodford, afterwards Scott County, north and east of the Kentucky River. There was also a small colony of Catholics, composed principally of Durbin and Logsdon families, settled in Madison County.^{PAGE 69}

Reverend Robert Angier OSD was then charged with these Kentucky missions. He had arrived from the area that now encompasses Waldorf, Maryland. The immediate area around Waldorf, Maryland is ripe in history. In 1681, a fort was built on the Zachia Swamp, about four miles southeast of La Plata, to protect the Zachia Indians against the Senecas and Susquehannocks of the north. To this fort were brought the Piscataways when their village was in danger of attack from their common enemy. Governor Charles Calvert, writing to his brother, Lord Baltimore, spoke of his intent to build a residence "on his Lordship's Manor of Sachay"; in 1673, he wrote that the house was complete, and he proposed moving from Mattapony to Zachia for greater security. At first it was a mission attached to St. Ignatius Church at Chapel Point, which is the original Catholic foundation in Charles County and from which most of the other Catholic churches in the county took their origin. (The word "Zachia," spelled Zacchia, Zachaiah, Zakiah, Zekiah, or Sachay, means "where there is a bend.")

The Jesuit fathers from St. Thomas Manor served the congregation of Upper Zachia from 1700 to 1792, when Archbishop Carroll sent Father J. B. David, a Sulpician, and a refugee from the French Revolution, to care for the congregation. Father Robert Angier, O.P., a Dominican, was his successor from 1805 to 1807. From that time until 1816, the parish was cared for by Father John Henry, S.J., a Belgian Jesuit, Father Heath, S.J., and Father J. B. Cary, S.J. from St. Thomas Manor.

In 1816, Father Angier returned from Europe where he had gone to solicit financial help for his several parishes, and was again appointed pastor at Upper Zachia until 1825.

This church eventually was rebuilt on donated property and was dedicated in honor of St. Peter the Apostle on August 15, 1860. It was the church here that John Wilkes Booth passed on his infamous escape from Washington to the house of Dr. Samuel A. Mudd after the assassination of Abraham Lincoln. This church later became St. Peter's Catholic Church.

Reverend Robert Angier OSD's successor was Reverend Samuel H. Montgomery OSD, ordained in 1816. Important settlements were Madison County and Lexington in Fayette County. Madison County, sixteen miles above Boonesboro, was made up of a half dozen families:

> *Christopher Durbin and family of six sons and six daughters, most of whom were fully grown at the beginning of this century; Elisha Logsden with six sons and six daughters; Joshua Brown, Edward Logsden, Clement Howard and Spink.*

With here and there an exception, the early Catholic settlers of Madison County afterwards found homes in one or another of the other Catholic settlements of the State. The venerable Father Elisha J. Durbin, who was born in Madison County in the year 1800, and who, when a youth was a penitent of Father Angier, speaks of him with unstinted praise. PAGE 92

The following is taken from a letter by Father F. P. Kenrick, St. Pius, Scott County, August 14, 1827:

> "Of the four Sundays of the month, three I give to Scott County; and also all the great festivals. Lexington has the first Sunday of each month, unless some great festival occurs. In Scott I hear confessions on Saturdays and Sundays, on the eves of festivals, on the festivals themselves, and whenever else penitents apply. I go to Lexington on Saturday evening, and I leave after mass on Monday morning—hearing confessions until 10 o'clock on Sunday, then celebrating, afterwards preaching, and at 3 o'clock PM teaching and explaining the catechism. In Scott I teach the children from 9 to 10 on Saturday morning and on each church Sunday, I instruct the servants at 3 PM.
>
> "Madison county might be visited four times a year. The first congregation is on Little Otter Creek, twenty-one miles from

Lexington, on the Richmond road. You take the road corresponding to the Main street of Lexington, and continue on to Clay's Upper Ferry, observing that, about five miles from town, where the road forks, you take the one to the right. Two and a half miles further on, after having crossed the river, the road again forks, and you will take the one to the left, which you will continue until it leads you to the humble habitation of Edward Logsdon, the progenitor of more than two hundred descendants. You will here find vestments which, for their poor material are worthy of the Apostolic Age. I take every requisite with me, even the wine for celebrating, since it is often impossible to secure them in the neighborhoods visited.

"From Otter Creek you will be guided to Drowning Creek, sixteen miles distant, where you will be plainly and heartily welcomed by a famous controvertist, Mr. Philip Durbin, whose humble mansion, consisting of one apartment, will accommodate the priest and his own numerous family. I have kept church in this lowly dwelling twice."PAGE 97

Note: "Cassius Clay, an advanced emancipationist before the late Civil War, and since and now well known in Kentucky as a politician of liberal ideas, was B. J. Webb's fellow-pupil at St. Joseph's college previous to the date of Dr. Kenrick's letter."

CASSIUS CLAY
Photo courtesy http://www.trader-skis.com

Cassius Marcellus Clay was the son of Green Clay; the second cousin of Henry Clay; the brother of Brutus Junius Clay (1808-1878); and the father of Brutus Junius Clay (1847-1932). He was born in Madison County, Kentucky, October 19, 1810. He was a member of the Kentucky state house of representatives from 1835 until 1837, and again in 1840. He freed his own slaves in 1844 and edited the only Southern antislavery newspaper from 1845 to 1847. He was shot point-blank during a speech in 1843, but he survived. He used a Bowie knife to cut off the attacker's ear and nose and cut out one eye. He was tried for mayhem and found not guilty. He served in the U.S. Army during the Mexican War; and was a candidate for the Republican nomination for Vice-President in 1860. He served as U.S. Minister to Russia from 1861 to 1862 and again from 1863 to 1869. He returned to the United States in April 1862 and was appointed Major General of Volunteers in the Union Army during the Civil War but performed little duty. He resigned from this post in March 1863. He was probably the best-known Southern emancipationist. Clay died of kidney failure in Madison County, Kentucky July 22, 1903. Interment was at Richmond Cemetery, Richmond, Kentucky. (Information on Clay was obtained from *The Political Graveyard* Internet Web Site.) More can be found on this remarkable man in the book by H. Edward Richardson, *Cassius Marcellus Clay: firebrand of freedom*, Lexington, University Press of Kentucky, 1976.

After the retirement of Father Joseph Rogers, the missions of Breckenridge County were for two years without a resident pastor (1832). They were visited, however, as often as once a month, by either Reverend Elisha J. Durbin from Union County, or Reverend A. Degauquier from Grayson.^{PAGE 153}

(Page 232 mentions after 1814 ordinations were…Elisha J. Durbin…. Page 348 mentions Father David's seminarians…. Reverend Elisha J. Durbin…. Pages 363 through 372 contain the complete story of Father Durbin's missions.)

The Church of St. John on Rude's creek, a small structure of logs, was built by Father Nerinckx about 1812. The First Catholic residents were Cissell, Hayden, Roby, Norris, Samuel Durbin, Riney Alvey, Drury.^{PAGE 415}

One of Father Degauquier's congregations, St. John the evangelist on Sunfish creek in Edmundson County, was made up principally of families of the name of Durbin. A list of "heads of families" in the pastor's handwriting shows a recurrence of the name Durbin is at least to be regarded as singular: John Durbin, Jacob Durbin, Richard Durbin, John Durbin Jr., Robert Durbin, Christopher Durbin, Nicholas Durbin, Doctor John Durbin, Daniel Cinter, Joseph Logsdon, Thomas Hill, Simon Sales, Austin Jenkins, John Skeis. ^{PAGE 418}

There were few Catholics living in Meade County previous to 1820, but there was a church station at Flint Island, or near that point, as early as 1810. This was visited occasionally no doubt by both Father Badin and Father Nerinckx. In 1818, Father Nerinckx wrote a diary of a journey made by himself and newly ordained Reverend Robert A. Abell from Gethsemani in Nelson to Morganfield in Union County in which occurs the following entry:

> At St. Teresa's, Flint Island, where Father Abell preached, we were presented with 300 acres of land for a church, etc. After the appointment of Reverend Elisha J. Durbin to the missions of Western Kentucky in 1824, the mission of St. Teresa, next

to those of St. Anthony in Breckenridge and Sacred Heart in Union County, was certainly the most important in the entire district.PAGE 420

In 1826, Father Durbin induced the congregation to put up for its use a small log church; and this was attended by him not oftener than once a month most likely until 1839 when Reverend Charles I. Coomes was charged with the mission with residence at Flint Island.

After 1824 up to 1833, the Catholic people of Daviess County were visited at long intervals by Reverend Elisha J. Durbin, from Union County, or by one of his assistants. The first Catholic Church put up in the county, St. Lawrence, a poor log edifice, was erected in 1831.PAGE 427 The county of Henderson adjoins Daviess on the east, and it has a local history that would be found interesting if it were proper here to pursue it. Before 1840, the number of Catholic families residing in the county could have been represented by two numerals. These were visited, however, at long intervals by either Father Durbin or one of his assistants.PAGE 429

In 1863 the church of St. Louis was finished and dedicated. From then until 1866 it was under pastoral charge of Reverend William J. Dunn then the assistant of Reverend Elisha J. Durbin of the church of Sacred Heart in Union County. The few Catholics residing in McCracken County previous to that date were visited occasionally by Reverend Durbin. About 1834 a number of German Catholics settled. Paducah, at first an unimportant station served by Father Durbin and his assistants, has become a city in which Catholicity was making marked progress. In 1864 a lot of one and a half acres was secured for a church, and mainly through the exertions of Father Durbin, the first church of St. Francis de Sales was built upon it.PAGE 430

Previous to 1850 the number of Catholic families south of the Green and Barren Rivers and along the line of the Louisville and Nashville Railroad could have been counted on the fingers of one's hand. The building of the Louisville and Nashville Railroad, in the latter half of the decade ending with the year 1860, brought to the section of the country hundreds of Catholic laborers whose position in a religious point of view was pitiable in the extreme. Up to that time, the few Catholic families living in the district had been visited at long intervals by Reverend Elisha J. Durbin.PAGES 496, 497

The following is from Pages 363-372:

> "The flourishing condition of the Church in Union County, Kentucky is to be ascribed, in the first place, to the fact that the first Catholic settlers in the county had their religious training from parents and pastors who were thoroughly imbued

> with the true Catholic spirit. They were of the number of those who, in childhood and youth, had been taught in sacred things by such admirable instructors as Fathers Badin and Nerinckx, Fournier and Wilson, Fenwick and David. The work done by these men of God in their regard had been in no wise superficial and it was destined to remain and to be productive of fruits for both themselves and their children. IN THE SECOND PLACE, THE PASTOR (Father Durbin) SENT TO THEM IN 1824 WHEN THEY WERE THEMSELVES, SO TO SPEAK, NEW TO THE COUNTRY, WAS HIMSELF, AND NO LESS THAN THOSE WHOSE NAMES HAVE BEEN MENTIONED, A MAN WHO FULLY UNDERSTOOD THE GRAVE RESPONSIBILITIES OF HIS POSITION, WHOSE ZEAL WAS UNQUESTIONABLE, AND TO WHOM LABOR AND FATIGUE AND DISCOMFORT APPEARED AS TRIFLES WHEN HE MIGHT BY THEIR ACCEPTANCE SUBSERVE IN ANY DEGREE THE SPIRITUAL WELFARE OF OTHERS."
>
> Catholicity in Union County, and in all Southwestern Kentucky indeed, is to the present hour (1884) so intimately connected with the name and personal labors of Reverend Elisha J. Durbin, that the writer regards it here necessary, and as a preliminary to his account of that important mission, to present to his readers a short sketch of the life of this venerable and most meritorious priest.

Here's how Webb, on pages 369-370, summarized the life of Father Elisha John Durbin:

> It is doubtful if the history of missionary enterprise in the United States furnishes a parallel of continuous and long-sustained labor such as has marked the career of the present priest-patriarch of Kentucky, Rev. Elisha J. Durbin. Many, no doubt, have labored as strenuously, and some with equal or greater effect; but in these enervated nature demanded much sooner release from toil. After twenty-six years of such service, Father Badin found himself no longer able to bear its fatigues. The same is to be said of his co-laborer, Father Nerinckx. He fell at his post of duty after eighteen years of travail that must ever be regarded as marvellous. But neither of the missionaries named, nor any other in this country whose

history is known to the writer, was favored with such continuity of energy as has distinguished the still living Kentucky inheritor of their gifts of zeal and fortitude. The record, brought up to this year of grace 1883, is as instructive as it is wonderful. Sixty-one years a priest. Fifty of these years devoted to missionary duty over a district of country that covers one-third of the entire State, with its Catholic population scattered far apart, and he the only priest west of Louisville to break to these the Bread of Life. A single chapel of logs in all that wide expanse of country west of Breckinridge county that had title to the name of house of God, and one single school conducted by Catholic religious. Horseback journeyings that he was himself in the habit of reckoning at the average of two hundred miles a week. *All manner of discomforts and privations, from stress of weather, from hunger and thirst, from loss of sleep, and from the numberless accidents and delays that are inseparable from nomadism in a sparsely settled country.

*A reverend friend who was his assistant in 1856, tells me that this is no exaggeration, and that he has himself little doubt that Father Durbin's combined journeyings on horseback during the sixty-two years of his priesthood would be under-reckoned at 500,000 miles. When he was so favored by circumstance as to be enabled to say his office outside of his saddle, he would jestingly remark, that he was entitled to a dispensation from that special duty on the plea of infrequency.

Now let us proceed in the examination of the Know-Nothings and another prominent anti-Catholic organization.

Chapter 8

The Letter "K"

In the decade before the Civil War, there was a climate of violence in Louisville. The anti-immigrant "Bloody Monday" riot of August 6, 1855, took more than twenty lives. And a vigilante killing of four blacks at the Court House on May 14, 1857, caused a newspaper editor to write: "The law has been put to death."

Hard times in other parts of the world in the mid-1800s resulted in an influx of immigrants to the Louisville area, and with them came religious orders, especially Roman Catholic ones. Catholics were a small minority in Louisville, but they counted among their number most of the Irish and German immigrants who were tightening up the city's job market and stirring ire among nationalistic Louisville citizens. The low-paying jobs were going to the immigrants who were desperate to work.

Tensions were heightened. When a papal delegate visited in 1853, he was burned in effigy. When the mayor of Louisville, a member of the prestigious Speed family, converted to Roman Catholicism during this era, his political career was nearly ruined. The Know-Nothing political party was a temporary but strong presence in American politics at this time, and Louisville was ripe for such demagoguery.

Father Elisha J. Durbin was at the midpoint of his priestly career when these troubles began. Although I could find nothing to indicate his involvement, he must have certainly felt the anger of the crowds, or, at the very least he anguished over this uprising. The loss of life alone would have taken its mental toll on

Father Durbin's sensitivities. The turmoil happened within the geographical boundaries of his ministry, and therefore had a profound effect on him and the people he served.

In the following statement, the term Native Americans refers to the people who were here prior to the influx of the Catholic immigrants. The Federalists were the Native Americans of their day, and Know-Nothingism, as the latest and, because of its excesses, the most odious manifestation of the Native American spirit, may be said to have had its genesis in the prejudices nursed by the Federalists against foreign-born citizens and in their intolerance of their fellow citizens professing the Roman Catholic faith.

It may be added that Roman Catholics of Irish origin, whether native or foreign-born, were at all times the special object of Native American hostility, and that the "foreigners," called that with contempt, against whom the Know-Nothing denunciations were leveled, and who were to be excluded from the rights of citizenship, were for the most part Irish immigrants to the United States professing the Roman Catholic faith. This Native American spirit may be traced back to the very beginning of the National Government. In many of the colonies there were laws that forbade the practice of the Roman Catholic religion, and these laws remained on the Statute Books down to the time of the War of Independence.

Although the existence of the new party was generally known, and its political activities soon became manifest, all inquiries by outsiders respecting its organization and purpose, and especially as to the names of members, were met by those identified with the movement with the answer: "I don't know." That's how the party got its name.

The tragic civil unrest directed at German, Irish and Catholic immigrants that culminated in what became known as "Bloody Monday" in Louisville began in the 1850s. Earlier settlers, who called themselves "natives," became increasingly alarmed at the influx of mostly German and Irish immigrants. In 1854 immigration from Europe had reached 300,000 in New York alone. Several nativist parties were formed, one of which was the "Know-Nothings" which wanted newer immigrants kept out of public office and from voting; they supported Protestantism and were opposed to Catholics. Another party called itself the "Know-Somethings."

The anti-Catholic fervor boiled over one election day, Bloody Monday, August 6, 1855, when at least 22 Irish and German immigrants were shot in their neighborhoods, on the city streets and even on the courthouse lawn. At issue was the right to vote, which the Know-Nothings were denying to naturalized immigrants. Louisville Journal editor George Prentice did his part with editorials naming the Vatican "the prostitute of Satan," and calling for action. The new cathedral and St. Martin's Church would have been burned by angry mobs had Know-Nothing Mayor John Barbee not physically searched them with a group of men and announced the churches free of munitions. Mr. Barbee stood before the church and defied the rioting mob. "If you intend to burn this church, you will have to kill me first", were his words as he stood, unarmed before them, and indeed, they backed down and left. Ironically, the bloodshed helped Roman Catholics in the long run—by provoking sympathy and thus creating an atmosphere of tolerance that continues to this day.

During the half-century preceding the Know-Nothing era, the questions involved in that movement had been frequently agitated. Catholics and foreigners were denounced, mainly from Protestant pulpits, as enemies of the Republic. Books and newspapers calculated to inflame the passions of the mob against their Irish and Catholic neighbors were extensively circulated. Catholic bishops and priests were maligned, their religion misrepresented and ridiculed, and acts of violence were committed against Catholics and their property. The burning of the Convent of the Ursuline nuns at Charleston, Massachusetts in 1834 by a Native American mob, and their cruel treatment of the unoffending nuns and their pupils, were the most notable manifestations, up to that time, of the evil effect of religious hatred.

Bloody riots also occurred at Philadelphia in 1844, when several Catholic churches were attacked by the Native American mob, and two of them, St. Michael's and St. Augustine's, were deliberately reduced to ashes, and the safety of those that remained was so endangered by the hostile demonstrations of the mob that public worship was suspended by order of Bishop Kenrick, and on Sunday, May 12, 1844, all Catholic churches in that city were closed. Many houses tenanted by Irish Catholics were likewise wantonly destroyed by fire, some of the inmates were shot down at their doorsteps, and a number of other unoffending citizens lost their lives.

In 1851 the large Know-Nothing element in Providence, Rhode Island, was excited over the establishment there of a community of Sisters of Mercy under the direction of Mother Xavier Warde. The cottage occupied by the sisters was attacked at night, and all the windows broken. In daytime, as the sisters passed through the streets, they were hooted at and otherwise insulted, and were openly threatened with the destruction of their convent. So persistent were these threats that the Mayor requested the sisters to abandon their residence in Providence so as to avert the threatened disorder. Soon afterwards a mob of Know-Nothing partisans, fully armed, was assembled whose purpose of attacking the convent had been openly announced. The bishop's house and one or more of the churches were likewise marked for destruction. After fruitless appeals to the civil authorities for protection, the Irish Catholics of

Providence, under the prudent and resolute lead of Bishop O'Reilly, prepared to resist the mob and to repel any violence that might be attempted. The mob marched to the convent, but, finding it guarded by a number of Catholic Irishmen, with Bishop O'Reilly present and declaring that the sisters and their convent should be protected at whatever cost, the Know-Nothing leaders decided not to molest the convent, and the mob dispersed.

At Cincinnati, in December, 1853, a mob of 600 men armed with weapons of various sorts, and carrying lighted torches and ropes, marched to the cathedral intending to set it on fire and, as was believed, to hang the visiting Archbishop Bedini, Apostolic Nuncio to the Court of Brazil. There was an encounter with the police, and the mob was dispersed, but not until after shots had been fired and several persons wounded. During 1854 there were numerous assaults upon Catholic churches throughout the country by the Know-Nothing element. St. Mary's church at Newark, N. J., was invaded by a mob made up of Know-Nothings and Orangemen from New York City; the windows were broken, some of the statuary destroyed, and one unoffending bystander, an Irish Catholic, was shot and killed. In October of the same year, at Ellsworth, Maine, Father John Bapst, S.J., was dragged from the church, robbed of his watch and money, tarred and feathered, and ridden about the village on a rail.

On July 4, at Manchester, New Hampshire, St. Anne's church was attacked, its windows broken and furniture destroyed, the priest compelled to seek shelter away from his home, and the houses of Irish Catholics were likewise attacked, the inmates driven out, even the sick being dragged from their beds. At Bath, Maine, the mob broke into the church and, after wrecking the altar and the pulpit, set fire to the building, which was reduced to a heap of ashes. At Dorchester, Massachusetts, a keg of gunpowder was placed under the floor of the little Catholic Church. It was set afire at three o'clock in the morning and this resulted in the almost total destruction of the building. Another Catholic church, at Sidney, Ohio, was blown up with gunpowder. At Massillon, Ohio, another church was burned, and an attempt made to burn the Ursuline Convent at Galveston, Texas. At Lawrence and at Chelsea, Massachusetts, the Know-Nothing mob attacked the Catholic churches, the windows smashed, and much other damage done. St. Mary's church at Norwalk, Connecticut, was set on fire and later its cross was sawed off the spire. A fire was started in the Church of Sts. Peter and Paul in Brooklyn, and the building was saved only by the interference of the police aided by the militia, who drove off the mob. St. Mary's Church at Saugerties, New York, was set on fire and nearly destroyed by the fanatics, and an attempt was made to burn the church at Palmyra, New York.

The following year (1855), at Louisville, Kentucky, the elections were attended with such rioting and bloodshed, the result of Know-Nothing agitation, that the day, August 6, acquired the name of "Bloody Monday". The cathedral was invaded by the mob and was saved from destruction only by the prudence of Bishop Spalding, who, in a letter to Bishop Kenrick summing up the results of the day's proceedings, said:

> We have just passed through a reign of terror surpassed only by the Philadelphia riots. Nearly one hundred poor Irish have been butchered or burned and some twenty houses have been consumed in the flames. The city authorities, all Know-Nothings, looked calmly on and they are now endeavoring to lay the blame on the Catholics. (see *Life of Archbishop Spalding*, by J.L. Spalding, p. 185).

The "Bloody Monday" mania took place within the territory of Father Durbin's ministry and it is quite likely that he lost some parishioners in the riots. And he may have even lost some of the churches he had built. We don't know for sure exactly what suffering he endured during this turmoil, but indeed there must have been *some* suffering.

Another politically inspired group that eventually would wreak havoc on American Catholics is the secret organization called the "Ku Klux Klan." Founded officially in December 1865 in Pulaski, Tennessee, near the Alabama border, by six former Confederate soldiers as a social club, it began to fill some of the void felt by these soldiers following their defeat in the Civil War. Begun eleven years before the death of Father Durbin, the organization probably didn't affect him much, except that it was founded in his large parish. Undoubtedly he wasn't very proud of this fact. Initially they were called "Kuklos" or "Kyklos" which is a word that comes from the Greek word for circle. By including the English word clan, the name became "Ku Klux Klan." A year after its founding the Klan leaders convened in Nashville, Tennessee to restructure the organization, both politically and racially. This new group originally had no political motivation, and when they donned their white clothes they played nighttime pranks.

The members of the new group, partly driven by the humor of it, named their leader the Grand Cyclops, while his assistant was the Grand Turk. The secretary was the Grand Scribe, Nighthawks were the messengers, and a Lictor was the guard. The future members, if they could find any, were to be called Ghouls. There was an initiation ceremony. New members would be blindfolded and told to repeat some silly oaths. He was subjected to some rough handling, then he was brought to a royal altar where he was to be given a royal crown. After the blindfold was removed, the candidate found himself looking into a mirror and wearing two large donkey's ears.

Since 1866 the Klan has gone by several names, including White Patriot Party, National Association of White People, White Aryan Resistance Party, Order of Pale Faces, Knights of the Rising Sun, Knights of White Camilia and Black Calvary of Alabama.

To some, the Klan was known as "The Invisible Empire of the South." The president was the Grand Wizard, with a descending hierarchy of Grand Dragons, Grand Titans and Grand Cyclopses. They covered their bodies with white sheets and placed white pillowcases over their heads. (Later tall pointed hats replaced the original headgear.) Often their horses wore white sheets too. This was done for several reasons. They thought their appearance would frighten superstitious folks. They felt the white garb would hide their identities from Federal troops. They dressed this way partly because of the humor of it all.

It is well known that the Ku Klux Klan hated Negroes. In furtherance of this hatred, they beat and otherwise tortured the black people, men and women alike, who were given their freedom after the war. In nighttime raids, they chased these former slaves and their white sympathizers out of town and/or they beat them mercilessly and/or they destroyed their crops and/or they burned their homes and barns. They even lynched some of the Negroes. All of this was done in the name of white supremacy. Some Klansmen served anonymously on county juries so they could influence the outcomes of cases against Negroes and Negro sympathizers. They also targeted Republicans and the schoolteachers who worked with Negroes. Branches of the Klan throughout the South had essentially the same basic goals, but they were loosely organized and there were great differences in their character.

In 1867, Nathan Bedford Forest, a former Confederate cavalry general, became the first Imperial Wizard and changed the group's focus to racism. Because things like kidnappings and murders were getting out of hand, Grand Wizard Forest ordered the Klan to disband in 1869. Because the racism and hatred were so ingrained in the minds of Klan members, the violence in the South continued. Those Klansmen who refused to give up succeeded in keeping blacks from going to the polling places to vote or from exercising any of the rights they had won at the end of the Civil War. They protested against black universities. The rest of the country finally turned its ire toward the Klan, and in 1870 Congress passed the Force Act, which allowed the President to use federal troops against the Klan, and in 1871 it passed the Ku Klux Klan Act. Initially, when Klansmen were prosecuted under the Klan Act, there was widespread Southern sympathy. Eventually, however, people of the South became more democratic in their thinking and in their politics. The violence subsided. Was this the final fate of the Ku Klux Klan?

The anti-Catholic bias really began 28 years after the death of Father Durbin, so he really didn't witness or experience their wrath against Catholics. In 1915, at Stone Mountain near Atlanta, Georgia William J. Simmons, a minister of the Methodist Episcopal Church and a practicing physician, rallied enough white supremacy sympathizers to resurrect the Ku Klux Klan. Simmons was also a veteran of the Spanish American War, and he was a salesman. It was Simmons who established the symbol of burning the cross at their outdoor meetings and claimed it to be a symbol of Jesus Christ being the light of the world. In fact, at the 1915 meeting at Stone Mountain, Simmons lit a match to a cross made of pine boards. The "new" Klan's activity peaked in the 1920s. With this new beginning, the Klan grew popular in the Midwest as well as the South, and, in addition to their racial bias, they added biases against Catholics, Jews, foreigners and labor unions. The Klan especially didn't want any Catholics to hold any governmental office. The Ku Klux Klan is still active to this day. (*The New Encyclopaedia Britannica Micropaedia*, 15th Edition.)

Father Durbin was often compared with another pioneer priest, Pierre-Jean De Smet, and perhaps it would be timely to include a sketch of Father De Smet.

REVEREND FATHER ELISHA JOHN DURBIN (1800-1887)

Chapter 9

Pierre-Jean De Smet

Pierre-Jean De Smet was a missionary among the North American Indians. He was born at Termonde (Dendermonde), Belgium, January 30, 1801. He died at St. Louis, Missouri, U.S.A., May 23, 1873. He emigrated to the United States in 1821 through a desire for missionary labors, and entered the Jesuit novitiate at Whitemarsh, Maryland. In 1823, however, at the suggestion of the United States Government a new Jesuit establishment was determined on and located at Florissant near St. Louis, Missouri, for work among the Indians. De Smet was among the pioneers and thus became one of the founders of the Missouri Province of the Society of Jesus.

His first missionary tour among the red men was in 1838 when he founded St. Joseph's Mission at Council Bluffs for the Pottawatomies. At this time also he visited the Sioux to arrange a peace between them and the Pottawatomies, the first of his peace missions. What may be called his life work did not begin, however, until 1840 when he set out for the Flathead country in the Far Northwest. As early as 1831, some Rocky Mountain Indians, influenced by Iroquois descendants of converts of one hundred and fifty years before, had made a trip to St. Louis begging for a "black-robe". Their request could not be complied with at the time. Curiously enough, the incident excited Protestant missionary enterprise, owing to the wide dissemination of a mythical speech of one of the delegation expressing the disappointment of the Indians at not finding the Bible in St. Louis. Four Indian delegations in succession were dispatched from the Rocky

Mountains to St. Louis to beg for "black-robes" and the last one, in 1839, composed of some Iroquois who dwelt among the Flatheads*and Nez Percês*, was successful. Father De Smet was assigned to the task and found his life work.

He set out for the Rocky Mountain country in 1840 and his reception by the Flatheads and the Pend d'Oreilles*was an augury of the great power over the red men, which was to characterize his career. (Augury is an ancient form of divination. The term "augury" probably refers to the practice of the Greeks and Romans to foretell future events by the observation and interpretation of the flights, chattering or singing of birds.) Having imparted instruction, surveyed the field, and promised a permanent mission he returned to St. Louis; he visited the Crows*, Gros Ventres*, and other tribes on his way back, traveling 4,814 miles in all. In the following year he returned to the Flatheads with Father Nicholas Point and established St. Mary's Mission on the Bitter Root River, some thirty miles north of Missoula, visiting also the Coeur-d'Alênes*. Realizing the magnitude of the task before him, De Smet went to Europe in 1843 to solicit funds and workers, and in 1844 with new laborers for the missions, among them being six Sisters of Notre-Dame de Namur, he returned, rounding Cape Horn and casting anchor in the mouth of the Columbia River at Astoria. Two days after, De Smet went by canoe to Fort Vancouver to confer with Bishop Blanchet, and on his return founded St. Ignatius Mission among the Kalispels of the Bay*, who dwelt on Clark's Fork of the Columbia River, forty miles above its mouth. Ten years later the mission was transferred to its present site in Missoula County, Montana. (The names indicated with an asterisk -*- are Native American Indian Tribes of Western Montana.)

As the Blackfeet were a constant menace to other Indians for whom De Smet was laboring, he determined to influence them personally. This he accomplished in 1846 in the Yellowstone valley, where after a battle with the Crows, the Blackfeet respectfully listened to the "black-robe." He accompanied them to Fort Lewis in their own country where he induced them to conclude peace with the other Indians to whom they were hostile, and he left Father Point to found a mission among this formidable tribe. His return to St. Louis after an absence of three years and six months marks the end of his residence among the Indians, not from his own choice but by the arrangement of his religious superiors who assigned him to other work at St. Louis University. His coadjutors in his mission labors, Fathers Point, Mangarini, Nobili, Ravalli, De Bos, Adrian and Christian Hoecken, Joset and others, made De Smet's foundations permanent by dwelling among the converted tribes.

De Smet was now to enter upon a new phase of his career. Thus far his life might be called a private one, though crowded with stirring dangers from man and beast, from mountain and flood, and marked by the successful establishment of numerous stations over the Rocky Mountain region. But his almost inexplicable and seemingly instantaneous ascendancy over every tribe with which he came in contact, and his writings which had made him famous in both hemispheres, caused the United States Government to look to him for help in its difficulties with the red men, and to invest him with a public character. Henceforth he was to aid the Indians by pleading their cause before European nations and by becoming their intermediary at Washington. In 1851 owing to the influx of whites into California and Oregon, the Indians had grown restless and hostile. A general congress of tribes was determined on, and was held in the Creek Valley near Fort Laramie, and the Government requested De Smet's presence as pacificator. He made the long journey and his presence soothed the ten thousand Indians at the council and brought about a satisfactory understanding.

In 1858 he accompanied General Harney as a chaplain in his expedition against the Utah Mormons, at the close of which campaign the Government requested him to accompany the same officer to Oregon and Washington Territories, where, it was feared, an uprising of the Indians would soon take place. Here again his presence had the desired effect, for the Indians loved him and trusted him implicitly. A visit to the Sioux country at the beginning of the Civil War convinced him that a serious situation confronted the Government. The Indians rose in rebellion in August 1862, and at the request of the government De Smet made a tour of the Northwest. When he found that a punitive expedition had been determined on, he refused to lend to it the sanction of his presence. The condition of affairs becoming more critical, the government again appealed to him in 1867 to go to the red men, who were enraged by white men's perfidy and cruelty, and endeavor to bring them back to peace and submission, and prevent as far as possible the destruction of property and the murder of the whites. Accordingly he set out for the Upper Missouri, interviewing thousands of Indians on his way, and receiving delegations from the most hostile tribes, but before the Peace Commission could deal with them, he was obliged to return to St. Louis, where he was taken seriously ill.

In 1868, however, he again started on what Chittenden calls (*Life, Letters and Travels of Pierre Jean De Smet*, page 92), "the most important mission of his whole career." He traveled with the Peace Commissioners for some time, but later determined to penetrate alone into the very camp of the hostile Sioux. General Stanley says (ibid.): "Father De Smet alone of the entire white race could penetrate to these cruel savages and return safe and sound." The missionary crossed the Bad Lands, and reached the main Sioux camp of some five thousand warriors under the leadership of Sitting Bull. He was received with extraordinary enthusiasm. His counsels were at once agreed to, and representatives sent to meet the Peace Commission. All the chiefs signed a treaty of peace July 2, 1868. This result has been looked on as the most remarkable event in the history of the Indian wars. Once again, in 1870, he visited the Indians, to arrange for a mission among the Sioux. In such a crowded life allusion can be made only to the principal events. His strange adventures among the red men, his conversions and plantings of missions, his explorations and scientific observations may be studied in detail in his writings. On behalf of the Indians he crossed the ocean nineteen times, visiting popes, kings, and presidents, and traversing almost every European land. By actual calculation he traveled 180,000 miles on his errands of charity.

His writings are numerous and vivid in descriptive power, rich in anecdote, and form an important contribution to our knowledge of Indian manners, customs, superstitions, and traditions. Later explorers testify to the general correctness of their geographical observations, though scientific researches have since modified some minor details. Almost childlike in the cheerful buoyancy of his disposition, he preserved this characteristic to the end, though honored by statesmen and made Chevalier of the Order of Leopold by the King of the Belgians. That he was not wanting in personal courage is evidenced by many events in his wonderful career. Though he had frequent narrow escapes from death in his perilous travels, and often took his life in his hands when penetrating among hostile tribes, he never faltered. But his main title to fame is his extraordinary power over the Indians, a power no other man is said to have equaled. To give a list of the Indian tribes with whom he came in contact, and over whom he acquired an ascendancy, would be to enumerate almost all the tribes west of the Mississippi. Even Protestant writers declare him the sincerest friend the Indians ever had. The effects of his work for them were not permanent to the extent that he had planned, solely because the Indians have been swept away or engulfed by the white settlers of the Northwest. If circumstances had allowed it, the reductions of Paraguay (see NOTE) would have found a counterpart in North America. The archives of St. Louis University contain all the originals of De Smet's writings known to be extant. Among these is the *Linton Album,* containing his itinerary from 1821 to the year of his death, also specimens of various Indian dialects, legends, poems, etc. The principal works of Father De Smet are: *Letters and Sketches, with a Narrative of a Year's Residence among the Indian Tribes of the Rocky Mountains* (Philadelphia, 1843), translated into French, German, Dutch, and Italian; *Oregon Missions and Travels over the Rocky Mountains in 1845-46* (New York, 1847), translated into French and Flemish; *Voyage au grand désert en 1851* (Brussels, 1853); *Western Missions and Missionaries* (New York, 1863), translated into French; and *New Indian Sketches* (New York, 1865).

Primary references for the story of Pierre-Jean De Smet follow: WILLIAM H.W. FANNING; transcribed by William R. McKenzie, in honor of Captain Joseph La Barge, friend of Father De Smet; CHITTENDEN AND RICHARDSON, *Life,*

Letters and Travels of Pierre Jean De Smet, S.J. (New York, 1905). It contains many hitherto unpublished letters and a map of De Smet's travels; DEYNOODT, P. J. De Smet, *missionaire Belge aux Etas-Unis* (Brussels, 1878); PALLANDINO, *Indian and White in the Northwest* (Baltimore, 1894); U.S. CATHOLIC HISTORICAL SOCIETY, *Historical Records and Studies* (New York, 1907), VII.; *The Catholic Encyclopedia, Volume IV Online Edition,* Copyright © 1999 by Kevin Knight.

> NOTE: Altogether the Jesuits in Paraguay founded approximately 100 Reductions, some of which were later destroyed; 46 were established between 1638 and 1768. Until 1767 new Reductions were continually being formed, while a constant stream of converts gained by the missionaries on their extensive apostolic journeys kept pouring into the older Reductions. Between 1610 and 1768, 702,086 Indians of the Guaraní tribes alone were baptized. The founding and preservation of these Reductions were the fruit of a century and a half of toil and heroic sacrifice in the battle against the terrors of the wilderness and the indolence and fickleness of a primitive people, as well as against the reckless policy of exploitation followed by the Spaniards, to whom the Reductions were ever an eyesore. Down to 1764 twenty-nine Jesuits of Paraguay suffered death by martyrdom. The Reductions were almost always laid out in healthy, high locations, the great central stations, as for instance Candelaria and Yapeyu, on the large waterways (Paraná and Uruguay) of the country. The general plan was similar to that of the Spanish *pueblos.* The Reduction was square, all streets running in straight lines, the main streets frequently being paved. The latter gave upon the *plaza* the large square where the church was situated generally shaded by trees and ornamented with a large cross, a statue of the Virgin and frequently also with a pretty village well; at the head of the *plaza* stood the church, and adjoining it, on one side, the residence of the Fathers, called the "College"; on the other, the cemetery, enclosed by a wall with a pillared hall *(The Catholic Encyclopedia).*

We shall now turn to the final days of Father Durbin's ministry.

Chapter 10

▼

The Sunset

"Father Durbin is as vigorous as ever...He may live in his usefulness yet many years. His hope of surmounting all his difficulties before he dies is as unbroken as ever" wrote Reverend William J. Dunn in 1867 to Archbishop Spalding. Reverend Dunn was previously an assistant to Father Durbin. In his effort to ensure that the story of Father Durbin's life would be preserved, W. Jesse Durbin wrote the following sketch.

> Life sketch of Reverend Father Elisha John Durbin as attested to by various sources and chronicles or historical accounts of his zealous missionary course showing the vastness of the field under his jurisdiction, his love of the priesthood and his zeal for the frontier missionary apostolate. Presented to Sister Loretta of the Ursuline Order of Mount St. Joseph of Maple Mount, Kentucky, from the pen of W. J. Durbin. Following this briefing of the family line of Reverend Father Elisha J. Durbin we shall now turn to his tremendous frontier missionary apostolate and the eulogies contributed to his memory.
>
> Elisha J. Durbin, son of John D. and Patience (Logsdon) Durbin, was born in Madison County, Kentucky, Feb. 1, 1800 and died at Shelbyville, Shelby County, Kentucky March 22,

1887. He was ordained to the priesthood at Bardstown, Nelson County, Kentucky by Bishop David on Sept. 21, 1822.

In 1873 Father Durbin was relieved of his pastoral responsibilities in Union County and given (at his insistence for pastoral service) all of the Catholic people living along the Elizabethtown and Paducah railroad, with headquarters in Princeton, in Caldwell County. Here he remained, laboring with much zeal and efficiency until a few years ago, when he was prevailed upon by his bishop to retire from active duties of the ministry and spend the remaining years of his life at the College of St. Joseph, in Bardstown. Of all his faculties, his memory appears to be the only one that age has seriously affected. He is still able to say his daily mass, (1884) and at no former period of his life was his heart more readily assailable than now on occasions that call for sympathy and personal service. He is surrounded in his retirement by those who consider it an honor to be permitted to minister to his wants, and thither followed him the love and veneration of all Western Kentucky, so far as it is Catholic.

After Hon. Webb had written the closing paragraph of his chronicle above, he tells us that he has learned, "that this venerable priest, now in his 85th year of his age and the 62nd of his ministry, has successfully sought from his ordinary leave to return to active duty in a section that once formed a part of the immense field upon which he had expended the energies of his prime. A more wonderful exhibition than this, whether of zeal or vital force, has not been witnessed in the territory of the United States."

The following article is taken from a brief sketch which appeared in a western paper, the Catholic Register perhaps, and submitted through the courtesy of Mrs. Nora McMahon (now Mrs. Mayo) of Albuquerque and Socorro, New Mexico about 1960.

Heroes of Christ

This pioneer Priest outranked even the fabulous Father DeSmet in the extent of his frontier journeyings. They earned for him the epithet of "Apostle of Western Kentucky" and "Patriarch-Priest of Kentucky."

Father Durbin was given the care of western and southwestern Kentucky, about one-third of the state. Then he began a missionary-career of over sixty years, hardly paralleled in the United States.

He rode a total of 500,000 miles on horseback, stopping at log-cabin churches, eating at farmers' houses after hearing confessions the whole morning; often his only fare was corn bread, salt pork and water.

The above article was accompanied by a photo of the young Father Durbin in his riding garb before mounting his steed and also after he had mounted in the act of making his departure. He was wearing a mustache and beard on that occasion.

The following chronicle appeared in the Catholic Register and a reprint from it in February, 1959 by the Reverend John B. Ebel. (One of a series of Catholic Builders of Our Land).

Side by side with the legendary Daniel Boones and Davy Crocketts who opened up the vast tangled wilderness of the Western frontier to settlement in the early 1800s were heroic priest-missionaries of at least equal stature. When the forests of Kentucky became the new frontier soon after the close of the Revolutionary War, many Catholics from Maryland established settlements in the wilderness. It was to serve these scattered congregations that a breed of wilderness missionaries grew up whose like has seldom been seen before or since.

One of these frontier priests, and among the most amazing missionaries in the history of the United States, was the Reverend Elisha John Durbin. Father Durbin earned for himself the title "Apostle of Western Kentucky" and "Patriarch-Priest of Kentucky." It is said that he traveled more than 500,000 miles on horseback. His mission covered 11,000 square miles of territory. From his center in Union County he journeyed over his vast territory, erected churches, established stations, formed congregations and visited isolated families.

Born February 1, 1800 in Madison County, Kentucky, Father Durbin was the son of John D. Durbin and Patience Logsdon. John D. Durbin in turn was the son of Christopher Durbin, one of the earliest pioneers of the state of Kentucky.

In 1816 young Durbin entered the preparatory Seminary of St. Thomas in Nelson County, where he studied under such distinguished missionaries as Bishop Benedict J. Flaget, S. S.; Co-adjutor Bishop John B. David, S. S.; Father Felix DeAndreis, C. M. As was customary in those days of frontier life, he spent about half of this time in manual labor at the institution, contributing to its support.

From there the young student went to the nearby Seminary of St. Joseph in Bardstown, where in 1821-22 he had as instructor Father Francis Patrick Kenrick, a distinguished theologian who later became Bishop of Philadelphia and Archbishop of Baltimore. Father Durbin was ordained to the priesthood Sept. 21, 1822, by Bishop David, who had been named Coadjutor of Bardstown in 1819.

For a year after ordination, Father Durbin was stationed at St. Joseph's Seminary and the Cathedral at Bardstown, where he assisted. Handicapped by extreme diffidence, he made little immediate impression on the people.

The young Priest was accosted soon after his ordination by a crusty old non-Catholic general, who bluntly stated: 'your people, Durbin, tell me you can't preach.' In an attempt to disprove the charge, the young Priest mounted the pulpit in the Cathedral shortly afterwards, but had scarcely begun before he lost track of his subject and after a few stammering sentences retired in confusion. The presence of the general in the congregation probably did little to help."

(Note: Hon. Webb asserts that the general was seated in a front pew at the appointed day for the sermon, and after the services he met Father Durbin and said he had one compliment to make upon his sermon—it was short. W. J. D.). Reverend Ebel proceeds.

The people in time, however, came to appreciate Father Durbin's single-hearted devotion to duty, his love of the ministry, and his constant labors in their behalf.

Conditions on the frontier

Conditions in the Kentucky missions of those days were described by the Reverend Felix DeAndreis, C. M. soon after arrival at St. Thomas, in Kentucky, Nov. 22, 1816. Father DeAndreis, another fabulous pioneer priest whose sanctity has led to consideration of his cause for the beatification, in a letter home told how the frontier priest must be constantly on horseback winding his way along the trails among the thick woods, sometimes 30 to 90 miles to visit the sick or attend various congregations.

The churches, Father DeAndreis noted were constructed of logs, without ornamentation, and were scattered in the woods. At the churches on festival days both Catholics and Protestants gathered from 20 miles around. At these times the woods were filled with horses, 'neighing as if a regiment of cavalry were in the vicinity.'

The mass, sermon, confessions and baptisms on one of these visitations could take the whole day. Describing the country around St. Thomas, he said there were 'neither towns or villages.' Men, women and children, of every age, came on horseback as far as 15 miles to attend mass, and if they received communion sometimes had to remain fasting until they returned home in the evening.

In those days of frontier hospitality, the priests on their missionary trips were welcomed and given food and lodging by the planters, eager to receive visitors. Even Protestants will do all in their power to receive him well, though the best fare he can expect consists of nothing but some corn bread very badly baked, salt pork, potatoes and water.

This is the refreshment that the missionary finds after a long journey, having heard confessions the whole morning until one or two o'clock in the afternoon, said mass, preached, baptized, etc.; sometimes at 5 o'clock in the evening he is still fasting.

This, then, was the life that the zealous Father Durbin endured for 60 years."

Work in the Missions

When Father Durbin was given charge of the Tennessee missions late in 1834 or early 1835, however, a brighter day dawned for the Catholics of the state. The little brick church in Nashville, unused since the time of Father Cosgrove, was in a dilapidated condition, and rather than put his parishioners to the expense of repairing it Father Durbin offered mass in the homes of the people. Thus it is said that he 'kept church' in the home of Philip Callagan.

Father Durbin would advertise his coming visits in articles in the press. Thus in <u>Catholic Advocate</u> of August 6, 1836 he informs the Catholics of Tennessee that he will shortly visit the state. His present intention is to be in Nashville on the third Sunday in October. He will also visit Gallatin and Hartsville. Catholics residing in other parts of the state will please meet him in Nashville, or let him know, as soon as possible, their places of residence, that he may call on them.

The city of Nashville, Tennessee and a few other scattered Catholic families in Tennessee had been having great difficulty obtaining the ministrations of a priest. A substantial brick church was completed in Nashville about 1830, but soon afterwards the congregation lost its pastor, the Reverend Thomas Cosgrove. For the next few years the Catholics were visited but intermittently, and made appeals far and wide for assistance. So when Father Durbin was given charge of the missions a brighter day dawned for them, repeated here for transition by the writer.

As Father Durbin continued to make his semi-annual visits to Tennessee in 1836 or 1837, a movement was in motion to make the state a separate diocese. He was happy to learn in the summer of 1837 that the diocese of Nashville, comprising the entire state of Tennessee, had been erected, with his friend Father Richard Pius Miles, Dominican Provincial, as its first Bishop.

"In 1824," relates the <u>Centenary of Catholicity</u>, "Father Durbin was entrusted with the pastoral care of the entire population of Catholics of western and southwestern Kentucky with headquarters near Morganfield in Union County."

His pastoral jurisdiction covered thousands of miles of territory, in every portion of which there were living at least isolated families, every one of whom was dependent upon him for spiritual aid and comfort, and to whose calls, in cases of sickness, prompt response was considered by him as of imperative obligation.

This immense field, it would reasonably seem, was beyond the powers of any unit of human capability to cultivate properly; and yet the Catholics living in the tier of counties that bordered the northern bank of the Ohio, in the states of Illinois and Indiana, were equally with his own people dependent upon him in all emergencies affecting their needs.

Besides all this, from and after the year 1832, the terms of his pastorate obliged him, once in the year at least, to visit Nashville, in the state of Tennessee, and to bear thither, to the few families there residing, the benefits of his ministry.

At this point in the discussion the writer wishes to digress in order to supply three recent discoveries that substantiate, in a certain degree, the verity of the last clause above.

From Ernest F. Schuchert the writer has been supplied, in a communication bearing date February, 1966, with the following data regarding Father Durbin.

Born in Madison County, KY 1800 died in March, 1887. First resident priest at Shawneetown, Illinois 1859. Had sole charge of Illinois as far north as Vandalia. Served 37 years in southern Illinois. Buried in St. Louis Cemetery Louisville, Kentucky.

(Note: Evidently 1859 is an error and possibly meant for 1839. This residence was obviously temporary headquarters of Father Durbin while attending the missions of Illinois. W. J. D.).

Historical sketch

Through the courtesy of Mrs. Louis Paul (Leona Ann Logue) Schneiter, late of Taylorville, Illinois in a communication under date March 17, 1961 the writer was supplied with the following account taken from the "Golden Jubilee" booklet presented to Mrs. Schneiter by the Reverend Father McKeogh when she visited him in quest of records for the "History of the Logues" which she and her cousin, Mrs. Mabel Joanna (Logue) Hopkins, were compiling. Historical sketch follows.

St. Clair's jubilee, Altamont, Illinois 1925.

Writing of St. Claire's Parish, that is including the mission place: the first priest to read Holy Mass in the parish was Reverend Father E. J. Durbin of Kentucky, in the year 1839. It has been related to me by Joseph Durbin, an early settler who met and conversed with Father Durbin, that the priest visited his scattered flock twice a year. He generally rode a white horse. This mission place was called Howard's Point, Mrs. Schneiter related.

As added proof that Father Durbin did attend at Howard's Point at St. Elmo, in Fayette County Illinois, and at St. Claire, in Effingham County, Illinois, Mrs. Schneiter in her exchanges on May 29, 1961, generously submitted the following article, quoted from the International Encyclopedia.

After a sketch of a John Price Durbin, Methodist minister, language college professor, etc. 1800-1876, it states that "His contemporary in Kentucky was Father Elishsa Durbin, son of blind John D. Durbin. Father Durbin was the first priest to say mass in St. Claire Church at Altamont."

After quoting Father Durbin's letter as given on page 21 Reverend John B. Ebel continues:

To prepare for the coming of the Bishop, Father Durbin arrived in Nashville in the summer of 1837, took up a collection, and had the church repaired and readied for services once again. Bishop Miles was consecrated September 16, 1838 in St. Joseph's Cathedral, Bardstown, and Father Durbin was one of the two priests present when he was installed in the Nashville church Oct. 14.

After guiding Bishop Miles on a 500-mile tour of the eastern portion of the state, Father Durbin returned to his post in Morganfield, Kentucky. His work in Tennessee was finished, except perhaps for occasionally urgent sick call, but he was to carry on his tremendous frontier missionary apostolate until death.

Enfeebled by age, his hardy constitution gave way in 1884, and Father Durbin was assigned to the small mission of Princeton, Kentucky. After a stroke of paralysis, he was given the chaplainship of an academy at Shelbyville, Kentucky in 1885, and died there in 1887.

The foregoing serial of testimonial chronicles are presented here as fitting tribute to the memory of one, like Father Durbin, who has spent so many years in persevering service to God and man. All honor to those who follow in a like cause, and to the venerable Elisha J. Durbin.

Supplementary concluding remarks by the writer:

"At the time of Father Durbin's demise in 1887, the academy where he assisted as chaplain was conducted by Mother Mary Agnes Mooney as we learn from Hon. Webb in his 'Centennial of Catholicity in Kentucky,' and was known as "Our Lady of Angels Academy." On Feb. 10, 1947, the writer wrote to the superior of said academy and was favored by a letter in reply from the rector of the church at Shelbyville that their small parish church and rectory was the only church property there. He was unable to give any information in reply to the questions in said letter. However he advised that: "the academy was sold about fifty years ago and the sister moved to a western city—Denver I believe. Since then there has been no Catholic school here. All the property, you see, belonged to the nuns, and was, therefore, in no sense parochial."

Mother Mary Agnes Mooney (1852-1926), was named the fifth superior of the congregation when only 26 years old. She led the congregation for 22 years, presiding over the tumultuous moves to Iowa and then finally to Clinton. Her brother was the acclaimed Indian expert, James Mooney.

Now we continue the story.

By 1872 nearly all the churches Father Durbin assisted in establishing had obtained resident pastors. This left a reduced Kentucky mission territory lying roughly between the Tidewater and Tennessee Rivers. In early 1873 he resigned his pastorate at Sacred Heart Church to devote his life to his remaining mission territory. Enfeebled by age, his hardy constitution gave way in 1884, and Father Durbin was assigned to the small mission of Princeton, Kentucky, where he purchased property for a church and attended the Catholics scattered through Caldwell, Livingston, Crittenden, Lyon, and Trigg Counties for the next eight years (Hawlett, *Historical Tribute to St. Thomas Seminary*, St. Louis, 1906).

In January 1881, Bishop McCloskey removed the zealous old priest, then in his eighty-first year, from the hardships of the missions in Union County and appointed him chaplain at St. Vincent Academy in Union County. Only a few months later he moved to Louisville as chaplain at SS. Mary and Elizabeth Hospital (12th Street). He was given (at his insistence for pastoral service) all of the Catholic people living along the Elizabethtown and Paducah railroad, with headquarters in Princeton, in Caldwell County. Here he remained, laboring with much zeal and efficiency until a few years before his death, when the Bishop appointed him chaplain at St. Vincent Academy in Union County in January 1881. A few months later, he moved to Louisville to become chaplain at Saints Mary and Elizabeth Hospital on 12th Street, and in November 1882, he took up his home at St. Joseph College, Bardstown.

Says the aged Father Durbin:

> There was no settlement of Catholics on Panther Creek when I was in charge of Daviess County 52 years ago in 1823. There were three families, the men non-Catholic, near where St. Lawrence stands fifteen miles above Owensboro. There was no Catholic settlement where St. Raphael and St. Alphonsus congregations are today.

(This was taken from the life story of Reverend Charles Nerinckx, who founded the Loretto Convent and Academy in 1812. It is located on Cox's Creek, at 37.4 miles on the road of Nazareth Junior College and Academy, founded in 1814. The library contains rare volumes. Its first home was a log cabin containing a table and wooden benches. Sister Anne was the first Mother Superior. In 1824 the convent was moved to St. Stephen's Farm, the former home of Reverend Theodore Badin, co-founder with Father Nerinckx of Catholicism in Kentucky.)

This venerable priest, in the 85th year of his age and the 62nd of his ministry, had successfully sought from his ordinary leave to return to active duty in a section that once formed a part of the immense field upon which he had expended the energies of his prime. A more wonderful exhibition than this, whether of zeal or vital force, has not been witnessed in the territory of the United States.

Of all his faculties, his memory appeared to be the only thing that age has seriously affected. In 1884 he was still able to say his daily Mass, and at no former period of his life was his heart more readily assailable than on occasions that called for sympathy and personal service. He was surrounded in his retirement by those who considered it an honor to be permitted to minister to his wants, and thither followed him the love and veneration of all Western Kentucky, so far as it is Catholic (*The Centenary of Catholicity in Kentucky*).

> But a better day dawns for the lonely missionary; not that it brings him longer intervals of rest, but that he is able to discover by its light that his labor has not been vainly expended. He has imbued his people with something of his own spirit. His admonitions are not only listened to, but they are having the effect to draw men's minds to a more careful consideration of their spiritual needs. There is to be seen among them more of charity and piety and practical religion, and it requires less of persuasion to induce them to spend their money for objects that are promotive of religious sentiment. Here and there an unpretensious church or chapel appears in the perspective with the Christian's emblem lifted above its modest belfry.
>
> And now the eyes of the missionary are gladdened by the sight of a priestly co-worker, and his thoughts are with his distant missions, hitherto visited so rarely becanse of his inability to be in two places at one time. In the meantime, with the revolving years and cycles, where there was at first but a single Catholic family, there are now clusters of them, and where the congregations were small, they are now large. His hands and those of his co-worker are kept busy in a narrowed circle, and he might be in despair because of the impending spiritual desolation of hundreds now cut off from his ministrations, were he not sustained by the unfailing influence of the

Church, working from the outside of his central field of labor, now relieving him of the care of one, and now of another, of his farther removed outlying missions. He has still enough to do, all of which mortal hands are capable. His rides are not so extended, to be sure, but his lank figure and bronzed face are as frequently seen on the road. He organizes congregations and builds churches. He takes thought of the rising generation, and multiplies his resources for its more perfect Christian culture and training. He follows the straying sheep and brings them back to the fold. In a word, he strives to render his ministry acceptable in God's sight and in that of his people. And thus ran the stream of his ministry for half a century, interrupted only at its close by the conviction, on the part of his bishop, that the limit of his strength had been reached, and that it would be a cruel exaction to require at his hands further exhibitions of his indomitable zeal (*The Centenary of Catholicity in Kentucky*).

Cathedral of the Assumption

On January 10th he received a severe stroke of paralysis by which for two weeks he was prostrated, but towards the middle of February he was so recovered that he was able to perform his duties as before. On March 20th he had intended to celebrate a Missa Contata, and to come down to the altar rail to give Holy Communion, and to preach a longer sermon than he had been able to deliver for two months. He fulfilled his intentions, and sang at vespers and administered Benediction.

After the stroke of paralysis, he was given the chaplainship at the Motherhouse and Academy of the Sisters of the Third Order of St. Francis at Shelbyville, Kentucky in 1885 and he died there March 22, 1887, in the sixty-fifth year of his ordination. Following the funeral services at the Cathedral of the Assumption, the mortal remains of the patriarch of the Church in western Kentucky were laid to rest in St. Louis Cemetery, Louisville (from Bishops and Priests of the Diocese of Bardstown).

The following is taken from a clipping in the Record found in a scrap book.

On Saturday March 19, 1887, Father Durbin wrote the Bishop (McCloskey) stating that the communicants were now obliged to approach the altar platform, as his weakness prevented him from going down the steps. When the Bishop received the letter Father Durbin was dead.

On Sunday, March 20, he celebrated High Mass and gave Communion at the railing, preached a sermon, sang Vespers, and administered Benediction.

On Tuesday, March 22, he said Mass and gave Communion at 6:00 o'clock, went for the mail at 11:00 a.m. and after dinner as usual paid a visit to the Blessed Sacrament. At 6:00 p.m. he had tea and when rising to give thanks, he fell smitten by a second stroke of paralysis.

The pastor of Shelbyville reached him in time to administer the Sacraments. At 6:00 p.m. his saintly spirit fled to its heavenly home.

His funeral was conducted with solemn Requiem Mass at the Cathedral in Louisville, with the Bishop on his episcopal throne and all of the clergy of the city in the choir. The celebrant was Right Rev. M. Bouchet, V. G.; Rev. E. M. Bachman, deacon; Rev. E. Fitzgerald, sub-deacon; and Reverends L. G. Depper, H. J. Brady, P. M. J. Rock, William Dunn, and E. Lawler, assistants.

The Bishop delivered a touching sermon.

The body of Father Durbin was interred in St. Louis Cemetery, Louisville.

Priests present: Rev. J. J. Tierney of Henderson, Rev. M. Dillon of Uniontown, Rev. T. Kellenaers of St. Ambrose, Rev. G. Van Troostenberghe, Rev. Jerome, C. P., Rev. Wm. Hogarty, pastor.

There could have been no more appropriate venue for Father Durbin's funeral than that of the Cathedral of the Assumption. The Cathedral of the Assumption was completed in 1852 at a cost of approximately $70,000—equivalent in modern terms to approximately $22 million. As Louisville's first Cathedral at a time when the city was larger than both Washington, D.C., and Chicago, it was a source of great pride to the citizens who contributed to its building fund. Of those supporters, it was said,

> Their names will be written in the book of life, and God himself will prepare for them a reward exceedingly great in heaven."

Designed by William Keely, one of America's foremost church architects, the Cathedral's 287-foot tall soaring spire was then America's largest. Its graceful Gothic interior featured ribbed vaulted ceilings, side aisles covered in 6-pointed stars and clear side-aisle and clerestory windows. Visitors thrilled to the beautiful hand-painted stained glass window of the Coronation of Mary, an ornate marble altar containing gifts from King Louis Philippe of France, a handpainted ceiling mural, and four paintings given to Bishop Flaget by Pope Gregory XVI in 1836. It was a truly grand and imposing structure.

The Ceiling Fresco, photo courtesy of the Cathedral's Web Site

The Ceiling Fresco of The Assumed Virgin surrounded by cherubs, was discovered under no less than six coats of paint. Today, it has been painstakingly restored to its former beauty.

The Coronation Window is original to the Cathedral and is one of the oldest and largest hand-painted glass windows in the nation. Evidence suggests that it was repainted in 1865, underwent restoration in 1883, and was removed in 1912 to make way for a new Assumption window. It has been lovingly restored and replaced in its earlier position of prominence.

The Cathedral's ornate columns, pointed arches, and ceiling's ribbed vaulting are characteristic of the Gothic style in architecture. The over 8,000 ceiling stars are 24-karat gold leaf, placed at random on a field of blue. The ornate bosses in the ceiling were installed in the original Cathedral as a means of ventilation. The IHS monogram represents the name Jesus Christ in Greek, and the VM is the monogram for the Virgin Mary in Latin (Virgo Maria). The interior walls are painted, using a faux technique that creates the effect of limestone blocks. The Cathedral's floor is white oak tongue-in-groove planking. The original seating capacity of the Cathedral was 1,300, in oak pews with doors.

The Coronation Window, photo courtesy of the Cathedral's Web Site

Early on, the Cathedral housed an orphanage and an infirmary and was the original site of the modern-day Presentation Academy. Since its construction, the

Cathedral has filled its traditional role as seat of the Diocese and as an active parish. The community has gathered there during times of national mourning: after the assassinations of Presidents Lincoln and Kennedy, during the onset of the Mideast War, and as healing progresses, during the annual service for the victims and survivors of the Standard Gravure massacres.

As indicated previously, retirement did not suit Father Durbin and the last three years of his life were spent as chaplain at the Motherhouse and Academy of the Sisters of the Third Order of St. Francis at Shelbyville, where he died March 22, 1887, during the sixty-fifth year of his ordination.

Mother Mary Agnes Mooney had in her possession an extract from the Louisville Record, May 31, 1906, bearing on the missionary record of Father Elisha J. Durbin. She generously permitted W. Jesse Durbin to copy it, which reads as follows:

> The approaching sixtieth sacerdotal anniversary of the venerable Father Fuller, of New Albany, Indiana recalls to our mind the late patriarch-Priest of the diocese of Louisville, Father Elisha J. Durbin. That blessed missionary was one of the glories of the Church in Kentucky. Born in Kentucky in the year 1800, he was ordained in Kentucky in 1822, he died in Kentucky in 1887, after sixty-four years of continuous ministry, loved, revered and honored by all. Even in his eighty-seventh year he besought his Bishop to let him return to active duty in his former arduous missionary section of the diocese.

(Comment: Mother Mary Agnes stated to W. Jesse Durbin that Father Durbin broke down and shed tears when his Bishop disallowed him further active duty in the missionary field.)

W. Jesse Durbin wrote the following.

> In the early 1900s somewhere around 1912 to 1915, Mother Mary Agnes Mooney and her band drifted down to Clayton, Union County, New Mexico, from Colorado, where the writer met and knew them personally, but at the time was not conversant in regards to the academy mentioned above but later learned by reading Webb's history of Kentucky that the Mother Mary Agnes of Clayton, New Mexico, whom he had met was the Mother Mary Agnes Mooney who once conducted the "Our Lady of

Angels Academy" at Shelbyville Kentucky. Mother Mary Agnes conducted a convent at Clayton, New Mexico and taught parochial school there at first, then she built the hospital there and conducted it a few years. In time, because of failing memory due to advanced age, the Bishop relieved her of the hospital charge and the nuns returned to Colorado, Pueblo perhaps. Mother Mary Agnes indicated to the writer an arm on which Father Durbin died and she was ministering to him in his last fleeting moments. The memory of Father Durbin also evoked from her words of praise and endearment. With this repetition in reference about Mother Mary Agnes I am ending this treatise as this covers about all the writer has to offer at present.

W. J. Durbin

May you cherish the memory of Father Elisha J. Durbin as much as yours truly does.

Following is a copy of a letter that Father Durbin had sent to Mother Mary Agnes Moony.

Shelbyville, Oct. 19, 1886.

Dear Mother Mary Agnes:

Your very welcome letter is received by this day's mail. I shall not write to Knottsville, but to Fancy Farm. The skin above the knee, that had become sore by the continued application of the salve, is well. But the knee still hurts me. The doctor said there was danger of its becoming a running sore. I have not applied to him since Sunday 10th inst., when he said I need not apply longer the remedy for that sore. The hurting is principally in the joint. It hurts in making genuflection. But also at other times. The Sisters are taking all the care they can.

I need not say anything about the well. A little water seeps in, but no vein. It is I believe 20 feet deep. It is walled up. I need not say more.

Give my respects to inquiring friends, my love and blessing to the Sisters. Ask Father L. to see whether I left a small French dictionary, and if so bring with you.

Yours truly in the Lord,

E. J. Durbin

W. Jesse Durbin sent Dorothy (see NOTE at the end of this chapter) a copy of a clipping from the May 31, 1906 edition of the *Louisville Record*: "The approaching sixtieth sacerdotal anniversary of the venerable Father Fuller, of New Albany, Indiana recalls to our mind the late patriarch-Priest of the Diocese of Louisville. That blessed missionary, Father Elisha J. Durbin, was one of the glories of the Church in Kentucky. Born in Kentucky in the year 1800, he was ordained in Kentucky in 1822, he died in Kentucky in 1887, after sixty-four (actually 65) years of continuous ministry, loved, revered and honored by all. Even in his 87th year he besought his bishop to let him return to active duty in his former arduous missionary section of the Diocese."

Following is a letter from the Rector of the Church of the Annunciation at Shelbyville, Kentucky, addressed to William Jesse Durbin.

> Church of the Annunciation
>
> 105 Main Street, Shelbyville, KY   Jan. 26, 1952
>
> Dear Friend,
>
> Pardon the delay in answering your letter of Jan. 7th. Father Elisha J. Durbin died at Shelbyville on March 22, 1887 and was buried in St. Louis Cem., Louisville, KY.
>
> Vincent J. Manger

Mother Mary Agnes, on whose arm Father Durbin expired when she tenderly raised his head and shoulders from the pillow in his last fleeting moments, spoke of him in very endearing terms. The funeral services were held at the Cathedral of the Assumption, and the mortal body of this patriarch of the Church in western Kentucky was laid to rest in the St. Louis Cemetery, Louisville, Kentucky.

Following a somewhat torturous seminary life, Father Elisha John Durbin built churches and endured the rigors of travel on horseback for sixty-five years. This pioneer priest outranked even the fabulous and saintly Father De Smet in the extent of his frontier journeyings. They earned for him the epithet of *Apostle of Western Kentucky* and *Patriarch Priest of Kentucky* (Heroes of Christ—author not given).

In the *Diocesan News of the Record* of Saturday, Nov. 4, 1882, we find the following:

> The Venerable Father Durbin will reside in future at St. Joseph's College, Bardstown in the midst of his old friends and on the spot where more than sixty years ago he was

ordained a priest by Bishop Flaget. Here, too, he will be able to aid his brethren of the clergy by preaching and saying Mass for pastors of the neighboring parishes, for though venerable in years, Father Durbin has much of the vigor and activity of youth.

Now we may say that his was a glorious life. From its commencement to its end, straight as the arrows flight and as stayless as the course. He sowed the good seed widely midst danger, and long watching and toil, and he nursed and tended its growth, with a continuous vigilance unexampled, and a force of endurance that never tired.

Simple in his habits, for him there were not the sustaining aids of luxury. Sickness seemed to have passed him by. Illness touched him never and he never seemed to have need of rest. He had even on earth his reward. It was given to him, to see with mortal eyes, how great was the result of his labors. It may have been given to him to feel as did the Apostle of the Gentiles, "I have fought a good fight, I have finished my course, I have kept the faith, as to the rest there is laid up for me a crown of Justice."

By 1872, fifteen priests were in the missions he had attended alone, each one of them having a large congregation.

> The little seed had grown
> Till to a great tree it spread;
> Other seed it brought forth
> Telling the story of the Dead.

The following obituary appeared in the *St. Joseph's Advocate* newspaper sent by Mother Mary Paul Carrico, Mt. St. Clare, Clinton Iowa, Feb. 7, 1939.

One of our warmest friends in Kentucky, as respects this "Advocate", is gone to his reward. We have given his likeness before out of sheer gratitude and pride, the permissable pride of pointing to the Kentucky Patriarch, going on ninety years, as a patron and active agent of this paper. That capital bust appeared in our issue of July, 1884. We said then that if he "survive the few years yet remaining of the 19th century he can claim a living, personal connection with three centuries."

The truth of this is apparent from the date of his birth, February 1, 1800.

We now honor his memory with a new illustration in the new attitude of a Franciscan Tertiary. For the last two years and a half he has been resident chaplain at the Franciscan Convent of Our Lady at Shelbyville, where he has been revered, loved and cared for as a Father, and where, to identify himself as much as possible with his spiritual children, even in externals, he assumed (after due investment of course) the outward garb, in which he is represented above, wearing the Cord of St. Francis.

The following is from the Funeral Oration by Bishop McCloskey.

We have to record our loss, the loss of a loved, venerable and self-sacrificing priest. To us has come the loss; to him arrived the time for eternal reward. The old ties binding the lives of our citizens to the birth of our century are rapidly, by death, being severed, and now but few, and very few remain. We desire to give a brief, and we regret necessarily, imperfect notice of the sacerdotal career of the venerable deceased.

Through the countless square miles, the sphere of Father Durbin embraced, lay scattered hamlets inhabited by professors of the faith. Here and there isolated individual Catholics were stationed long, long miles apart, whilst in many places roads were but a dream of the future, not advanced enough to be a hope, and often danger lay along the course. All these were ministered to by Father Durbin as we have said unaided and alone. How did he perform the duty? Almost ever on horseback, from long before dawn until long after the day had past, often riding to remote distances in the darkness of the night. He was undeterred by fiercest blizzards and unstayed by treacherous snow-wreath and the nipping frost never left his energies uncontrolled.

He loved his people, he was affable to everyone, approachable by all; his sternness was exhibited only in the merciless demands he made on his own mental powers, and physical frame. His recollections of faces was extraordinary; he knew personally his flock, and for each had ever the cheering word and kindly greeting.

No surprise that they reverenced and loved him and still no surprise that respect was spontaneously yielded to him by those without the fold. Amidst the parishioners of his vast domain he watched and prayed for fifty years, and even when having reached some three years past the allotted span, his iron frame began to feel the effects of his almost superhuman toil, still he strove gallantly on. His Bishop hearing of his over-taxed strength and 'knowing that there was a time for all things,' wrote to Father Durbin that now for him, it should be one of rest. He wished him to remain at the Cathedral, but Father Durbin, as Elisha of old, was unwilling to lay aside the duty upon the performance of which he had set his heart. He grew feebler and feebler in frame. At length he recognized that he should relinquish the charge of the beloved parish he had served so long and so well.

He received instead parochial charge of the Catholics at Princeton, Ky., and those along the line of rail from Elizabethtown to Paducah. Growing feebler still, he retired from active life, and decided to spend the remaining years at St. Joseph's College, Bardstown, close by the Church where he was ordained past fifty years gone by, and which college was rich to him in memories of the first years of his priesthood.

Yet another obituary appeared in the *Record* newspaper Feb. 7, 1885:

The venerable Father Durbin celebrated his 85th birthday at Shelbyville. Rev. Wm. Dunn, who had been his assistant at Sacred Heart, was present.

The day being Sunday prevented many clerical friends of Father Durbin from participating in the joyous festivity and wishing him a still more extended term of years in which to shed the light of his priestly example and his salutary counsels of the faithful.

In the Sacred Heart Church of Union County there is an altar erected in memory of Father Durbin by Rev. William Hogarty.

A slab bearing these words greets you as you enter the Church: "A greatful people have erected the high altar and the niches of the Church in memory of Father Durbin's self sacrifice and zeal for their welfare."

Pray for the soul of Father Durbin.

Born Feb. 1, 1800. Died March 20, 1887.

For 49 years pastor of this congregation.

Let priests who serve well be esteemed worthy of double honor.

The burial on Thursday morning, from the Cathedral, was numerously attended by the clergy of the city and convenient points of the diocese. The Mass of Requiem was celebrated by Vicar-General Bouchet. Bishop McCloskey delivered the funeral discourse in which the life and labours of this conspicuous pioneer Priest were depicted in affecting terms. The interment took place at St. Louis Cemetery.

Here's another newspaper obituary dated April 2, 1887:

DEATH OF FATHER DURBIN

Rev. Elisha Durbin, a pioneer priest of Kentucky, and the second oldest priest in the United States, died Tuesday, March 22, in Shelbyville, at the age of 87 years.

The octogenarian Father came in with the century. He was born at Richmond, Madison County, Ky., February 1, 1800, ordained priest at Bardstown September 21, 1822, and for 65 years has labored as such in this diocese. He was one of the pioneer priests of Kentucky who, at the cost of much hardship and privation, cleared the ground and planted the mustard seed which has grown to be the wide-spreading tree of today.

In 1824 he was sent to Morganfield, in Union County, then embracing a circuit of 150 miles. About the time he reached his seventieth year he often became very weak from heart disease. Several times he fell from his horse while making his rounds. Repeatedly had the Bishop invited him, in view of his great age, to retire from the constant labor of the pastorate, before he could bring himself to give up his beloved parish. He then took charge of a church at Princeton, Ky., and after a few years went to Bardstown. He next came to this city and was for a while chaplain of the Sts. Mary & Elizabeth Hospital. About three years ago he went to Shelbyville and ministered to the Sisters until his death, of old age, on Tuesday the 22nd ult.

The burial Thursday morning from the Cathedral was numerously attended by the clergy of the city and convenient points of the diocese. The Mass of Requiem was celebrated by Vicar General M. Bouchet. Bishop McCloskey delivered the funeral discourse. The interment took place in St. Louis Cemetery.

Following is an article copied from The Western Watchman—April 9, 1887—St.. Louis, Missouri.

DEATH CLAIMS REVEREND ELISHA J. DURBIN

After a long and useful life for sixty-five years in the service of the Lord.

We have to record our loss, the loss of the beloved, venerable and self-sacrificing priest. To us have come the loss; to him, arrived the time for eternal reward. The old ties binding us in the lives of our citizens to the birth of our century are rapidly, by death, being severed, and now but few, and very few, remain. We desire to give a brief, and we regret necessarily, imperfect notice of the early life and sacerdotal career of the venerated deceased.

Continuous exercise, in manual labor inured him whilst yet in early youth to the endurance of great and prolonged strain on his physical powers. He eagerly grasped the limited educational advantages afforded where he was brought up, and we learn throughout his stay under the paternal roof of his unselfishness, docility and obedience.

We know how the fateful revolution in France wracked many a school of theology, and desecrated many a shrine; how the saintly Benedict J. Flaget (afterwards our first bishop), with others, left his native land for the cause of the faith, reached Baltimore, and with the pious Fathers David and Badin, in a floatboat, descended the Ohio to the falls; it is perhaps needless to recall, 'that flatboat was at once the cradle of the seminary and the Church in Kentucky.' Our noble Cathedral is a fitting monument to Bishop Flaget.

Father Badin is remembered as the Apostle of Kentucky, and the first seminary within its limits arose under the eye of that illustrious Sulpician, Father David, who afterwards, in 1819, was consecrated Bishop of Mauricastro. To this first seminary, cradled in the flatboat on the Ohio, we find John Durbin and his wife in 1816, at his earnest solicitations take their pious son Elisha. He was impelled to the Seminary of St. Thomas by a vocation from above.

The course in the seminary presented no holiday time to the young Levites. Half their hours were devoted to study, the other half to the labors in the field, the duties of the workshop, or to such other toil called for by needs of the institution. The discipline was rigid; food plain and drink unvaryingly water.

The young Elisha was undepressed by the difficulties of study; there was in his spirit an ever-renewing spring impelling him forward; it was not his to falter or look behind. For six years he remained at the Seminary, and on the twenty-first day of September, 1822 region was placed beneath his pastoral charge. Let us look at it on the map. On the one side, the Ohio, on another, Tennessee, on the east the western line of the county of Jefferson, and on the west of the Mississippi. This territory lay within his charge, but it did not limit the domain of his spiritual stewardship. Across the Ohio it was his to attend the Catholics of Illinois, and for many a season, in addition, had he to minister to the faithful, then few, at Nashville, Tenn., and this all unaided and all alone, for many a year.

Providence fits men for the exigencies which arise and the necessities which they are to meet.

Through the countless square miles the sphere of Father Durbin embraced lay scattered hamlets inhabited by professors of the faith. Here and there isolated individual Catholics were stationed long, long miles apart, whilst in many places, roads were but a dream of the future, not advanced enough to be a hope, and often danger lay along the course.

These, all these, in every sorrow, in the loosening of the chains of the penitent, in breaking the Bread of Life, in the regenerating of the newest come to earth, or composing and absolving the departing, and in the need of every priestly care were ministered to by Father Durbin, as we have said before, unaided and all alone.

His center of operations, so to speak, was at Morganfield, Union county, Ky. How did he perform the duty? Almost ever on horseback, from long before dawn until long after day had done, and sometimes far into the night. He crossed the Ohio in every kind of weather, in frail boats; his hours of sleep took but little from his hours of action, and they were irregularly and fitfully enjoyed. He was undeterred by fiercest blizzard, and unstayed by treacherous snow-wreath, and the nipping frost left his energies uncontrolled.

He was undiscouraged by length of travel, where the path lay lost, or where intervening distances precluded refreshment or repose. The sacred call of duty was sounded, it was ever responded to; nor was Father Durbin ever reluctant, or tardy, or aught but joyous in the performance of its behests. His journeys on horse-back never told less than two hundred miles a week. Absolute rest he had none. His resting time was spent in the confessionals in the celebration of the Holy Sacrifices in the various duties which make demands upon a priest, and in collecting means, and in striving and endeavoring to erect fitting temples for the worship of God.

In physique, he was a man above the middle stature, lithe, and vigorous of frame. In early years he was of pleasant manner and appearance, but long exposure to inclemencies of weather, had tanned his complexion, and almost gnarled his features.

As a preacher, the Reverend Father would not have been classed high among the schools where tawdry eloquence, garish sensuousness and kaleidoscopic doctrine obtain honor, but he was pervaded with the apostolic spirit and his doctrine according to the Rock of Peter, had been impressed indelibly upon his youthful mind by the lectures of that eminent theologian, Bishop David, and he had at all times reason for the faith that was in him.

As we have mentioned, his residence was at Morganfield. There in the year 1820, the Community of the Sisters of Charity of Nazareth had founded the Academy of St. Vincent. On their grounds they erected a log hut chapel. It was the only place, on the arrival of Father Durbin, to offer up the Divine Sacrifice. He at once girded himself to the holy work, but relaxed not a moment of his other labors, he girded himself to erect a fitting temple. It rose beneath his care, and stood close by the site of the old log chapel on the grounds of the Sisters of Charity. It was dedicated to the Sacred Heart. In the year 1828, on the fourteenth day of September, the anniversary of the Exaltation of the Holy Cross, it was blessed by the Right Rev. Benedict J. Flaget, then Bishop of Bardstown. It was blessed when the Rev. Father had reached the 28th year of his age, and the sixth of his ordination.

The Catholic population of the district had increased, and required more visitation, and spiritual succor was needed in places where Catholics had not been before. Still his round of duties was the same.

He afterwards set his heart on building a church at Fancy Farm, in Graves county. He strove with hope to build it, his energy was crowned with success and he saw it blessed under the invocation of St. Jerome, in the year 1836.

In the course of time, the flock, small upon his arrival at Morganfield, and which had increased rapidly up to the building of the church in 1828, had so further increased in numbers as to need a more spacious edifice than that which succeeded the log hut chapel.

A new church of adequate dimensions was erected through the incessant efforts of Father Durbin. He loved his people, was affable to everyone, and approachable by all. His sternness was exhibited only in the demands he made upon his own powers and physical frame. His remembrance of faces was extraordinary; he knew every member of his flock personally, and had ever the cheerful and kindly greeting.

No surprise then, that all reverenced and loved him. No surprise, that all reverence and respect were yielded spontaneously to him by those without the fold. Amidst the pioneers of his great districts he watched and prayed for fifty years. Even when having passed the allotted times and the almost superhuman efforts began to tell on his human strength, he strove gallantly to keep up the good work.

His Ordinary heard of his over-tasked strength, and knowing that there is a time for all things, wrote to Father Durbin that for him it should be now. The Bishop wished that he would stay at the Cathedral in our city, but the Father, as Elisha of old, was unwilling to lay aside the works upon the performance of which he had set his heart.

He grew feeble and still more feeble in frame. At length it was recognized that he should relinquish his beloved parish which he had served so long and so well. He received instead the parochial charge of the Catholics at Princeton, Ky. There was at that time a line of rail from Elizabethtown to Paducah. Growing weaker still, at the request of his Bishop, he retired from active life, and decided to spend his remaining years at St. Joseph's College, Bardstown, close by the church where he was ordained past fifty years gone by, and which college was rich to him in memories of the first years of his priesthood. But for him, no more than there had been for St. Alphonsus, there was no time for idleness upon earth. He besought his Ordinary to be permitted to go once more into active duty. His Bishop did know how to refuse the glowing fervor in the aged priest.

We see him assigned to the chaplaincy of the Hospital of Sts. Mary and Elizabeth in our city. Leaving there we see him where he wrought his last work in the vineyard of the Master, chaplain at Shelbyville, Kentucky, Our Lady of the Angels Convent, in charge of a Community of Franciscan Sisters. A chaplain within the limits of that great territory where once he had served alone.

He continued to the last to celebrate the Holy Sacrifices though his strength was fading fast. On the 19th of March he wrote to his Bishop, "that the communicants were now obliged to approach him on the platform close to the altar, as his weakness prevented his going down the steps." The Bishop stated during the burial service, "that day he was dead." He died at Shelbyville.

NOTE: As a reminder, Dorothy May (Schmitzer) Durbin Breitenbach (1914-1990) is the mother of this author. Dorothy was an author in her own rite, having published numerous stories in Catholic and other publications, notably the *Catholic Weekly, Immaculata, Our Sunday Visitor, the Catholic Digest, Scope, The Christian, Grits, Guideposts, The Detroit News,* and *Good Old Days*. Besides devoting extensive time and effort to writing, she spent roughly thirty years of her life researching Durbin families. She developed a fascination with the historical significance of the Durbin name and had a burning desire to learn what made her husband, Donald Ross Durbin, "tick." In researching the Durbins, taking great pains to document and authenticate everything, she traveled to all the places where she knew there was some Durbin ancestry. Her research took her to such places as Kentucky, Ohio, Maryland, and even England.

DEDICATION

FATHER ELISHA DURBIN

In humble thanksgiving for the blessings God has bestowed upon our parish since its beginning, and in sincere appreciation of the hardships and difficulties encountered by the early settlers and especially by the missionary priests who ministered to them, we respectfully dedicate this program to the memory of Father Elisha Durbin, who labored so faithfully to nurture the spark of faith which he found in the home of John and Catherine Rebstock in 1847.

ST. POLYCARP PARISH

(This picture was on a dedication pamphlet of St. Polycarp Parish, Carmi, White County, Illinois)
REVEREND FATHER ELISHA JOHN DURBIN (1800-1887)

SOURCES

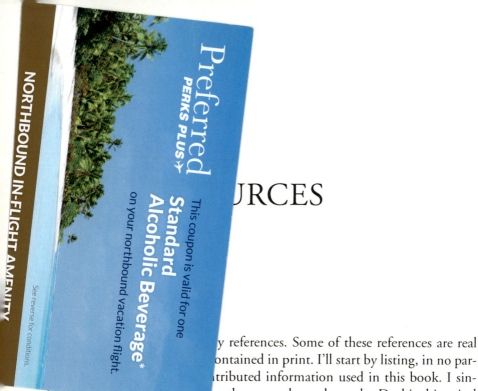

...y references. Some of these references are real ...ontained in print. I'll start by listing, in no par... ...tributed information used in this book. I sincerely appreci... ...ns these people made to the Durbin historical research, and particularly to this book.

- Mr. Steve Barr was a Durbin researcher who corresponded with Dorothy. Although there was a fair amount of correspondence between Mr. Barr and Dorothy, it is not known where, or even if, he fits into the Durbin family.
- Mr. W. (William) Jesse Durbin was a Durbin researcher who corresponded with Dorothy also. Jesse Durbin descended in a direct line from Christopher Durbin, the Kentucky pioneer, and he really should be the subject of his own book.

He grew up and went to school in Christian County, Illinois where he graduated from the eighth grade. His parents were farmers, and at age 28 he went to New Mexico. On July 24, 1908 he homesteaded on a half section of land in the Perico community, a few miles southeast of the small town of Mount Dora. He lived and farmed there for thirty-five years. He was also a carpenter, and was often asked to build the coffin when there was a death in the community. He also wrote poetry. He researched the Durbin and related families for 65 to 70 years of his life. He left his New Mexico farm in 1943, returning to his home state of Illinois where he continued his family research.

The last Dorothy heard, he was 93 years old and still living in 1973 in Morrisonville, Illinois. Due to intermarriages (cousins marrying cousins, etc.) he is all "Durbin" on both his mother's and father's sides (on his father's side through Christopher's sons Joseph and Edward "Ned" Durbin, and on his mother's side from "Stumpy John" Durbin and Solomon Meeds). He wrote to Dorothy that he had a second cousin, Paul Henry Durbin, living in Maryland not too far from Westminster at Hyattsville. Paul's mother and W. Jesse Durbin were cousins, and Paul's father and W. Jesse Durbin's father were cousins.

Jesse took no confirmation name. He never married and lived alone in a small house. He fell in love once, but she died quite young, and he never found anyone else to take her place. Dorothy referred to him as a "delightful old gentleman." She and her husband had visited with him, and they last heard from him in November 1972. They learned of his death when their 1974 birthday card to him was returned, marked "Deceased—Return to Sender." In 1974 he wrote to Dorothy from the Cottage Shelter Home, a nursing home in Raymond, Illinois. Dorothy made a note on his February 4, 1974 letter to her that in fact he was in the *Barry* Nursing Home in Raymond, Illinois.

In a letter dated January 23, 1974 to Dorothy, written from the nursing home, he mentioned that he sent his family records to a niece in St. Louis, Missouri, and to another niece in Albuquerque, New Mexico for safekeeping.

In his February 4, 1974 letter to Dorothy, he said, "I had a visitor yesterday, Jerry Durbin of Decatur, Illinois. I had never met him or his father but knew his grandfather in the 'Good Old Days.' His great-grandfather and I were first cousins.... Jerry is a nice young man some 31 years old, or maybe younger. He says he will call on me later. I didn't think to get his address. I got in touch with one Ronald Lee Logsdon of Kentucky, a descendant of our line. He and wife visited me and he borrowed some of my records, especially Welch's notes. As I do not have my records I can't explain the connection well so will not try."

He had exchanged genealogy records with many researchers, including E. C. Welch, Mrs. Florence (Durbin) Cole, Mrs. Evalou Gillock, J. J. Crider, and Mrs. Janette Henshaw. Mr. James R. Virden, himself a Durbin researcher who died in 1995, wrote a poetic tribute to honor W. Jesse Durbin:

We have all mourned the passing of this pious man,
in his lifes work of helping one another,
love came first, like grains of sand,
like his special way of loving his mother,
in all his thoughts, prayers and deeds
Answer him, O God of love,
Meet him at the gates of Heaven and fulfill his needs.

Jesse passed this life, in the Holy month of May,
Entered the Heavens, Mary, Queen of Angels, leading the way,
Sent by God, his lifes work done,
Silent in death, as in his prayers of atone,
Enjoy his presence, he is no longer alone.
Dearly missed by all he loved and touched,
Under his guidance we all learned so much,
Raised by parents true servants of God and trust,
Blessed are they for sharing him with us,
In our life and death, in time to come,
Never forget this gentle man, for all the work he's done.
                                         James R. Virden

- Mrs. M. Evalou (Fisher) Gillock of Louisville, Kentucky spent her research on the Christopher Durbin line, and she said that Christopher, the Kentucky pioneer, came to Kentucky about 1785 after serving as a patriot in the Revolutionary War in Maryland. Like W. Jesse Durbin, she was also a descendant of Christopher Durbin.

- Mrs. Dorothy Thomas Cullen of the Filson Club, Louisville, Kentucky was another one of Dorothy Durbin's contacts that provided much information on the Durbin families in early Kentucky. (The Filson Club was organized May 15, 1884 for collecting, preserving and publishing historical material, especially that pertaining to Kentucky.)

- Mrs. Frank J. Stodden, Jr. (nee Virginia Lavern Stewart) was a Durbin researcher who corresponded with Dorothy. As with the above Steve Barr, it is not known exactly how she is related to the Durbin families. Coincidentally, Mrs. Stodden lived in Lafayette, Colorado. After the death of Dorothy Durbin's husband, Dorothy moved to Lafayette also and remarried there; however, this move took place many years after the correspondence with Mrs. Stodden stopped.

- Mrs. Jan Bell Linn, who lived in Palmdale, California, was a Durbin researcher who corresponded with Dorothy. I am not sure if this full name is correct because she only referred to herself as "Mrs. Jan Bell Linn." She is related to the Durbin families, descending from Perdilla Ann Durbin, daughter of Edward "Ned" Durbin. Ned Durbin was a great-grandson of Christopher Durbin, the Kentucky pioneer. Perdilla married Louis Crawford.

- Mr. James Virden, of Versailles, Ohio, corresponded with Dorothy. He had spent 20 years in California before moving back to Russia, Ohio in 1973. On May 1, 1978 he moved to Versailles, Ohio. As of 1978 he had complained to Dorothy of ill health at age 53. According to Dorothy's research notes, he's a cousin of Jesse Durbin, and a descendant of Thomas Logsdon, born 1710, through Edward, Prudence, and Ann. According to one of Dorothy's clippings, he received an award for traveling the longest distance to attend the 1978 26th reunion of the Durbin family in Taylorville, Illinois. On October 30, 1995, William P. Durbin, Jr. informed me of Jim's death. He said Jim was a wounded and disabled veteran of World War II.

- Carol Ann (Durbin) McKellar of Saginaw, Michigan corresponded much with Dorothy on the Durbin genealogy, and later she corresponded with Dorothy's son, Don, this author. Carol is Don Durbin's third cousin and their common ancestor is their great-grandfather, Basil Durbin. She was a retired Medical Assistant and has 4 children, 2 stepchildren and 13 grandchildren.

- Mr. Edwin C. Welch was a noted Durbin researcher and author who corresponded with Dorothy's husband, Donald, between 1944 and 1949. Mr. Welch also provided much information to W. Jesse Durbin and others. Mr. Welch had at least one son and one daughter (W. Jesse Durbin had a clipping about the son's marriage). Mr. Welch's strenuous research impaired his health and doctors told him to lay off research for a couple years. Mr. Welch is descended from either the Durbin or Logsdon families, but precisely where he fits in is a mystery to this writer.

- Luella Frye, who resided in Mount Vernon, Ohio, was a Durbin researcher who corresponded with Dorothy. She probably is a Durbin descendant, but it is not known just how she is related.

- Mr. Lawrence Hyter was a Durbin researcher who corresponded with Dorothy. Lawrence was a great grandson of Charity Durbin who married

Ephraim Washington Hyter. Charity is a great-granddaughter of William Durbin, son of Samuel and Ann Durbin.

- William Pius "Bill" Durbin, another family researcher, corresponded with this author from 1995 until February 2001, when Bill passed away. Bill was also one of the editors of *A Durbin Heritage*, a book by Robert Ross Durbin (see next paragraph). Bill had served in the United States Navy, then he retired after 32 years from the Defense Mapping Agency, Senior Executive Service, with very impressive credentials. He worked with many NATO countries and received numerous United States and foreign awards. He had been involved in the Minuteman and Trident missile programs, cruise missiles, and intelligence and tactical systems. As of 1995 he was doing consulting work in mapping and related fields. In 1958 he received his B.S. degree in Geology and Mathematics from St. Louis University and in 1959 he performed post-graduate studies in geodesy, geophysics and space sciences. He attended Air War College in 1970, and Industrial College of the Armed Forces in 1974 and was a distinguished graduate. He has other formal schooling as well. Bill and his wife, Lorraine had ten children. Bill descended from Christopher Durbin through Christopher's son John J. "Blind Johnny" Durbin. Father Elisha John Durbin, subject of this book, was a son of "Blind Johnny."

- Robert Ross "Ross" Durbin was a Durbin researcher, but this author knew little about his work until his book, *A Durbin Heritage*, was published in November 2000 and distributed following Ross' death in January 2001. (Ross was a brother of Max Durbin who had been Chief of Police in Flint, Michigan.) Ross lived in St. Louis, Missouri. Robert Ross Durbin is a great-great-great grandson of Christopher Durbin whose brother Thomas is this author's (Donald Ross Durbin) great-great-great grandfather. Ross had corresponded with Betty Jewell (Durbin) Carson, author of *Durbin and Logsdon Genealogy* and probably furnished her with information that appears in her book. Betty Carson's book was not used as a reference for this book about Father Durbin. However, *A Durbin Heritage* was used, with permission. William Pius Durbin wrote on April 5, 1996, "I hope Ross (St. Louis) publishes his Durbin Family records. He has been talking about it for nearly twenty years and is not in the best of health. He wrote me recently that he has a nephew in Texas who wants to pick up where he left off. Ross has done hard research, visiting cemeteries in at least three states and confirming/modifying what many have taken for granted. He also worked closely with Jim Virden. I have a very rough draft of his paper

(probably about 150 or so pages which contains not only vital statistics but many family stories which make very interesting reading.)"

- Mary Ferguson Loher, a cousin of the above Ross Durbin, with her daughter Rebecca Sue Loher, gathered Ross Durbin's information and typed the initial manuscript of *A Durbin Heritage*. Mary also furnished the following items, all of which were used in this book:

    o Some of the writings of W. Jesse Durbin.

    o An article entitled "Horseback Priest" by Wendell Givens from *The Mayfield Messenger* newspaper dated March 22, 1987.

    o Written remembrances of Reverend J. M. Higgins of St. Vincent's in Union County, Kentucky.

    o An article entitled "Reverend Elisha J. Durbin—Death—Life Sketch" that appeared in *The Western Watchman* newspaper April 9, 1887, St. Louis, Missouri.

    o An article by Lucille Lawler in *The Messenger* newspaper January 4, 1985, found in the archives of Mount St. Joseph, Maple Mount, Kentucky.

Mary Loher's grandmother was Clara Loretta Durbin who married William Bartley. Clara's great grandfather was "Blind Johnny" Durbin, the father of Elisha John Durbin the saintly priest.

Following are the reference works I used in compiling this book:

- *The Centenary of Catholicity in Kentucky* by the Honorable Benjamin J. Webb. This illustrated book of 594 pages is considered a historical source book of more or less reliability.

- *History of Western Maryland* by Scharff

- Page 268, *Van Wert and Mercer Counties 1896 Biographical History*.

- Ref: Durbin family in *History of Union County, Kentucky, 1886*, page 317 (DAR Library, Washington, DC, November 1964):

- *Catholic Encyclopedia*, Volume 5 (Kalamazoo, Michigan Library).

- *Catholic Encyclopedia*, Volume 5 (Newberry Library, Chicago, Illinois).

- *Dictionary of Catholic Biography*, Delaney Tobin (Battle Creek, Michigan Public Library).
- *History of M. E. Church* by Abel Stevens, LLD, page 494.
- *Appleton Cyclopaedia of American Biography*, Volume II.
- *Life of Reverend Charles Nerinckx* by Maes (Newberry Library, Chicago, Illinois), pages 220, 525.
- *The New Encyclopaedia Britannica Micropaedia,* 15th Edition.
- Certain information about *The Star Spangled Banner* was taken from page 5 of the Music Workshop section of the March/April 1995 edition of *Sheet Music Magazine.*
- Additional references: *The Catholic Advocate* (Louisville 1836-1887); *The Record* (Louisville 1879-1887); Hawlett, *Historical Tribute to St. Thomas Seminary* (St. Louis 1906); *Catholic Builders of Our Land* (Rev. John B. Ebel); *Heroes of Christ* (author not given).
- A few Internet sites also provided some information, and these are mentioned together with the context they furnished.

978-0-595-30294-9
0-595-30294-7

CPSIA information can be obtained
at www.ICGtesting.com
Printed in the USA
LVOW11s0500261016
510316LV00001B/31/P

9 780595 302949